INTRODUCTION

QUICK WIN LEADERSHIP is aimed at both experienced and aspiring leaders who are looking for concise, yet informative, answers to the most frequently asked questions about the leadership role. In a meaningful way, the book explores complex issues related to leading others, providing simple and practical guidance which can be readily applied, regardless of your current level or seniority as a leader. For the new leader, it offers a roadmap to build your capacity and enhance your performance; for the old-hand, it provides an ideal opportunity to take stock and consider your talents in the light of some best practice leadership principles.

QUICK WIN LEADERSHIP is designed so that you can dip in and out of the content as the need arises to search for answers to your top leadership questions. There are five sections to the book:

- Leadership Essentials.
- Leadership Qualities.
- Leadership Skills.
- Leading Individuals and Teams.
- Leadership Activities.

Leadership Essentials covers some of the really fundamental questions that all leaders have regarding the role of leadership, such as how it relates to management, what leaders actually do, or whether the ability to lead others is limited to the select few or can be learned and developed by anyone.

Leadership Qualities focuses on questions that relate to the personal characteristics seen time and time again in the best leaders. It is more concerned with *who* leaders are than *what* it is they do and is designed to help you to consider your own strengths and areas for improvement in light of a better understanding of the attributes that support effective leadership.

Leadership Skills shifts the emphasis to what leaders do. Specifically, the questions in this section explore many of the common concerns that leaders have regarding the skills needed to get the best out of others. It provides helpful guidance on critical issues, such as how to communicate more effectively and how to apply different leadership styles.

Leading Individuals and Teams addresses a range of questions relating to everyday aspects of leading people at work. It provides useful answers to frequently raised questions, such as how to better engage your employees or how to deal with those really difficult individuals you meet from time to time.

Leadership Activities looks at some of the key organisation-wide activities undertaken by leaders, particularly those in more senior positions. It explores topics such as how to develop and implement strategy, manage performance or improve service delivery in a systematic way.

In addition, using the grid in the **Contents** section, you can search for questions and answers across a range of topics, including: behaviour, communication, management performance, strategy and planning, and theory. And, where appropriate, answers cross-reference to other questions for a fuller explanation or more information.

Enjoy the book – I wish you lots of quick wins and success in your leadership role!

> **Enda Larkin**
> **Geneva**
> **September 2010**

LEADERSHIP

Answers to your top 100 leadership questions

Enda Larkin

Published by
OAK TREE PRESS
19 Rutland Street, Cork, Ireland
www.oaktreepress.com

A catalogue record of this book is
available from the British Library.

ISBN 978 1 904887 47 8

CONTENTS

Search by theme:

Or search by topic:

Behaviour

Communication

Management

Performance

Strategy and Planning

Theory

using the grid overleaf.

LEADERSHIP ESSENTIALS

	Behaviour	Communication	Management	Performance	Strategy & Planning	Theory	Page
Q1 What is the relationship between leading and managing?			☑			☑	2
Q2 Why is leadership so important today?	☑						4
Q3 Is leadership relevant only to senior managers?	☑		☑				6
Q4 What is the relationship between leadership and power?	☑					☑	8
Q5 Can everyone lead?	☑					☑	10
Q6 Why is having a personal vision so important for leaders?					☑		11
Q7 How does a leader translate their vision into reality?					☑		13
Q8 Why is leading by example so critical?	☑	☑					15
Q9 Do leaders need to inspire others?	☑	☑					17
Q10 Which is more important for leaders – focusing on the people or the needs of the job?	☑		☑			☑	19
Q11 What do employees look for in a leader?	☑						22
Q12 Do leaders need to be liked in order to be successful?	☑						25
Q13 What are the most common mistakes that leaders make?	☑						27
Q14 Why is personal development so necessary for leaders?	☑						30

LEADERSHIP QUALITIES	Behaviour	Communication	Management	Performance	Strategy & Planning	Theory	Page
Q25 Why do leaders need to be self-motivated?	☑						52
Q26 Why do leaders need high levels of competence?	☑						53
Q27 Why is empathy important to a leader?	☑	☑					55
Q28 Why is integrity essential for leaders?	☑						57
Q29 Why is creativity so vital in a leadership role?	☑						59
Q30 How might I cope better with stress?	☑						61

LEADERSHIP SKILLS	Behaviour	Communication	Management	Performance	Strategy & Planning	Theory	Page
Q31 What are the main theories of leadership?	☑					☑	64
Q32 What are the different leadership styles?	☑					☑	66
Q33 What influences the style of leadership adopted by a leader?	☑					☑	69
Q34 How can a leader be flexible and adaptive without seeming inconsistent?	☑						71

LEADERSHIP SKILLS	Behaviour	Communication	Management	Performance	Strategy & Planning	Theory	Page
Q35 What are the core leadership skills that contribute to success?	☑					☑	73
Q36 Why is communication so important for leaders?	☑	☑					75
Q37 How can I communicate more effectively?	☑	☑					79
Q38 What are listening skills and why are they important?	☑	☑					84
Q39 Why are daily briefings important for leaders?	☑	☑					87
Q40 How can I manage meetings more effectively?	☑	☑	☑				90
Q41 Why are presentation skills so critical in a leadership role?	☑	☑					94
Q42 How can I write reports professionally?	☑	☑					98
Q43 How can I improve my negotiation skills?	☑	☑					100
Q44 Why are influencing and persuading skills important?	☑	☑					103
Q45 How can I develop my problem-solving skills?	☑	☑					106
Q46 How and when should I delegate?	☑	☑	☑				107
Q47 How can I become a better planner?	☑	☑					109

LEADERSHIP SKILLS	Behaviour	Communication	Management	Performance	Strategy & Planning	Theory	Page
Q48 How might I use mentoring and networking as tools to help me grow as a leader?	☑						111

LEADING INDIVIDUALS AND TEAMS	Behaviour	Communication	Management	Performance	Strategy & Planning	Theory	Page
Q49 What makes an effective team?	☑					☑	114
Q50 How do teams change and develop over time?	☑						116
Q51 What is the difference between organisation culture and climate?	☑					☑	119
Q52 How can I motivate and engage my team-members better?	☑	☑					121
Q53 How can I foster greater collaboration amongst my team-members?	☑	☑					123
Q54 How should I deal with difficult individuals in the team?	☑	☑					125
Q55 How should I handle employee grievances?	☑	☑	☑				127
Q56 How should I discipline team-members?	☑	☑	☑				129

LEADING INDIVIDUALS AND TEAMS	Behaviour	Communication	Management	Performance	Strategy & Planning	Theory	Page
Q57 How should I respond to the high-performers in my team?	☑	☑					132
Q58 How can I deal more effectively with conflict?	☑	☑	☑				134
Q59 How should I deliver feedback for best results?	☑	☑					137
Q60 How can I make my performance appraisals produce better results for me?	☑	☑	☑				140
Q61 How should I recognise and reward my employees?	☑	☑	☑				144
Q62 Why is training and developing my employees important?	☑						146
Q63 How should I coach my employees to improved performance?	☑	☑					149
Q64 Is counselling my employees something I should be doing?	☑						152
Q65 What is empowerment and how much autonomy should I give my employees?	☑						154
Q66 How should I manage employee diversity effectively?	☑		☑				156
Q67 How should I retain my best employees?	☑						158
Q68 Why are exit interviews important?	☑	☑					160
Q69 What should I look for when I recruit new team-members?	☑						162

LEADING INDIVIDUALS AND TEAMS	Behaviour	Communication	Management	Performance	Strategy & Planning	Theory	Page
Q70 How can I use the interview process more effectively to help me find the best people for my team?	☑	☑					164
Q71 What other tools can I use to help me select the best employees?	☑						167
Q72 Why is new employee induction so important to maintaining a positive team dynamic?	☑	☑					170
Q73 How should I monitor a new employee's performance?	☑			☑			172
Q74 Should I socialise with my team?	☑						174

KEY LEADERSHIP ACTIVITIES	Behaviour	Communication	Management	Performance	Strategy & Planning	Theory	Page
Q75 How do I achieve excellence in my organisation?	☑				☑		176
Q76 What is the strategic planning process?	☑				☑		178
Q77 Why are organisational vision, mission and values important?	☑				☑		180
Q78 How should vision, mission and values be developed?	☑				☑		182

KEY LEADERSHIP ACTIVITIES	Behaviour	Communication	Management	Performance	Strategy & Planning	Theory	Page
Q79 How should vision, mission and values be used for best effect?	☑	☑			☑		184
Q80 What analysis is important when strategic planning?	☑				☑		186
Q81 How can I conduct an effective SWOT analysis?	☑				☑		189
Q82 How should I develop and implement strategy?	☑				☑		191
Q83 How can I review strategic effectiveness?	☑			☑	☑		193
Q84 What is a leadership competence model?	☑					☑	195
Q85 How can I establish an effective system to manage human resources in the organisation?	☑		☑				198
Q86 What is employee engagement?	☑	☑					200
Q87 How can I increase employee engagement levels?	☑	☑					202
Q88 How might I measure employee engagement?	☑			☑			206
Q89 How can I establish a leadership mentoring programme within the organisation?	☑						209
Q90 What is performance management?			☑	☑			212
Q91 Why is succession planning important?					☑		215

KEY LEADERSHIP ACTIVITIES	Behaviour	Communication	Management	Performance	Strategy & Planning	Theory	Page
Q92 What is process mapping and how can it help improve business performance?				☑			217
Q93 How can I improve service delivery in the organisation?				☑			221
Q94 How can I apply the principles of continuous improvement within the organisation?					☑		223
Q95 What is benchmarking and why is it important?					☑		225
Q96 How can I encourage and manage innovation?					☑		228
Q97 How should I manage a crisis?	☑	☑	☑				230
Q98 How should I lead change for best results?	☑				☑		232
Q99 What is corporate social responsibility?			☑				235
Q100 How might I unify all the principles of leadership?	☑					☑	238

LEADERSHIP ESSENTIALS

Q1   What is the relationship between leading and managing?

There is a long-standing debate surrounding the relationship between leading and managing: some believe that leadership is a function of management, while others argue the opposite. On a day-to-day basis, the terms frequently are used interchangeably to mean the same thing. Nonetheless, it is important to understand how leadership and management interrelate, as it has implications for how you build your own capabilities as a leader.

In developing that understanding, it is helpful first to explore what is expected of someone holding a position of authority, at any level, in any organisation. Think of yourself here, or if not already in a leadership position, think of someone who is. On the one hand, to be successful, you must *achieve* results of some kind: increase customer satisfaction, control costs, deliver agreed revenue and profit targets, or whatever the expected outcomes might be. Yet, in any organisation, the quality of those results is always greatly influenced by the people who actually do the work; therefore, you also must *engage* your employees so that they are motivated to deliver to the best of their ability. Thus, being successful in any managerial position is largely dependent upon on how well you balance this *engage to achieve* dynamic.

In seeking to find the right balance, *managing* focuses on the 'hard' aspects of the role: planning, organising, controlling, budgeting and so on, whereas *leading* is concerned with the 'soft' aspects of work life or, in other words, the human dimension. Simply being able to manage – no matter how well you do it – is not enough today because, unless your employees are motivated and passionate about what they do, results ultimately will suffer. Equally, being a great leader who fully engages employees is of little value either, if that engagement is not translated into better results. Therefore, leading and managing should not be seen as either / or alternatives since, to succeed, you must be able to do both – and well – because they are interdependent. **QUICK WIN LEADERSHIP** uses the term 'leader' but always in the sense of someone who can both manage and lead.

The real challenge of effective leadership is having the right attributes and skills to help you to excel in both the management and leadership roles; it is never easy to be an all-rounder and this is why only a few very talented individuals combine the skills of leading and managing to best effect. Some are good at managing but find it hard to engage with people, which can lead to low morale and productivity; others can engage with employees, but they fail to turn that engagement into better results. Still, it is not an impossible task to find the right mix and you don't have to be superhuman to do so. It involves, in the first instance, understanding the skills and attributes required and then working hard to develop them over time.

See also

Q3   Is leadership relevant only to senior managers?
Q16   What personal attributes are required to be a successful leader?
Q86   What is employee engagement?

Q2   Why is leadership so important today?

Leadership gets more attention today, largely as a result of changing attitudes to work. Whereas, in the past, it may have been possible simply to tell employees what to do all the time, or to show little concern for them, that is no longer the case; the days when a boss said "Jump" and employees asked "How high?" are long gone. As employee attitudes to work and their expectations from it have evolved, the approaches taken to get the best from them naturally have had to adjust in response; what works today is different from what worked in the past, simply because people in general have changed.

Employees think very differently about work-life than they did, say, even 30 years ago, and the nature of work in organisations simply mirrors those changes. Today, the majority of employees expect more from their jobs and, indeed, from the relationship they have with their boss. People are generally more educated, have more employment rights and, perhaps most important, view work from a very different perspective than previous generations. For most people, work needs to be about something more compelling than just paying the bills, so they seek some sense of meaning from the positions they hold. As a result, on a day-to-day basis, they expect to be treated fairly, to have input into decision-making, and to work for someone whom they value and respect; they will not respond well to being 'managed' in a narrow sense where they are treated merely as implementers of the decisions taken by others. For this reason, leadership has grown in importance over recent decades as a proven response to these new realities. Research continually shows that, where leadership is weak, employee engagement, productivity, and overall work quality are lower than when leadership is strong.

Leading others, therefore, is about creating an environment that is inclusive and responsive to employee needs but, at the same time, remains totally focused on achieving the desired results. This is often one of the misconceptions about leadership, that it is somehow about creating a 'happiness camp' at work, or that it leads to a situation where the 'tail is wagging the dog'; it is about none of those things. Leadership means viewing your employees as partners but is just as concerned with the quality of outcomes. In that sense, effective leadership is good for both the employee and the organisation.

See also

Q1   What is the relationship between leading and managing?
Q13   What are the most common mistakes that leaders make?
Q16   What personal attributes are required to be a successful leader?

Q3   Is leadership relevant only to senior managers?

No, most certainly not. Leadership is essential at all levels of the organisation but how it is applied in practice differs depending upon the level involved. Senior leaders in organisations naturally get more attention – there are not too many books on leadership written by Joe who heads the sales team – but leaders at all levels have a vital role to play in helping the organisation to achieve its stated goals and objectives. The challenge of leadership, therefore, is organisation-wide.

At a senior level, leaders are responsible for defining and communicating an overall direction for the business or, in other words, its vision, mission, goals, and related strategy. These leaders also must ensure that the organisation has the right structure, people and culture in place to realise those goals and that all these components are mutually supportive. This is a vital role because no business can succeed without clear direction and the necessary systems, resources, and working environment to back it up. However, having a strategy is one thing; delivering on it is another matter entirely. It is the leaders, right throughout the organisation, who play an important role in bringing the goals to life:

- Leadership tasks at mid-level in the organisation cover the spectrum of activities necessary to ensure the business is moving in the right direction, as defined by those at the top.
- Leaders at the front-line must ensure that employees make the products or deliver the services to a high standard.

It is the effectiveness of this 'trickle-down' leadership model that separates the best companies from the rest of the pack. A strong, unified leadership team always outperforms a disjointed one.

A simple point regarding the challenge for leaders at the various levels often is overlooked. While senior leaders mainly interact with a small pool of people on a daily basis, most of whom are likely to be highly motivated given the positions they hold, leaders further down the chain of command must interact with the larger body of employees. This, in itself, creates its own challenge because, not only are there more people to deal with, they have differing motivation levels, ranging from high to low. So, from the perspective of getting the best out of people, the more junior leaders in the organisation arguably have the tougher task.

See also

Q6   Why is having a personal vision so important for leaders?
Q7   How does a leader translate their vision into reality?
Q16   What personal attributes are required to be a successful leader?
Q35   What are the core leadership skills that contribute to success?
Q77   Why are organisational vision, mission and values important?

Q4   What is the relationship between leadership and power?

Power frequently is seen as a dirty word, when in reality there is nothing wrong with having power; a leader, of any type, cannot succeed without it. However, it is in how power is applied that problems often arise. To understand better the relationship between leadership and power, consider it from two perspectives: where power comes from and how it is applied.

Where power comes from
Where your power comes from is important, as it has significant implications for your leadership style and your ability to build an effective team:

- **Formal** power is derived from the authority or power attached to a post or role; depending on your position, you have the right to direct the actions of others. Every leader in the workplace needs to have this designated authority, otherwise there would be no clear lines of control and, ultimately, chaos would ensue. However, over-reliance on this formal power potentially is a weakness, since the name badge does not the leader make today.

- **Informal** power is the form of authority that results from having special attributes, skills, or even expert knowledge. Others look up to you, not solely for the position you hold but because of what can be called your personal power.

Truly effective leaders are those who combine formal and informal power; they have the authority that goes with a certain position, but they also have the personal power that makes people look up to, and believe in, them. It could be said that 'management', or certainly old-style managers, relied too heavily on formal or positional power, whereas leadership is about using informal or personal power as one's main source of strength.

What some leaders often forget is that every group or team, over time, converges towards one leader, perhaps not the one nominated by authority; if you do not have personal power, someone else within your team may be the real leader.

How power is applied

In terms of how power is applied, there is a broad spectrum of approaches ranging from the power of *influence* to the power of *coercion*. The power of influence means that you have the skills and attributes necessary to attract people in the direction you want them to go; you can convince others of your way of thinking. Coercive power is the opposite, in the sense that you force people in the direction you want them to go, which in reality is not leadership at all. True leaders – because they have good personal power – operate most of the time at the influencing end of the power continuum; those who lack personal power end up closer to the coercive side. Of course, the realities of work mean that a bit of coercion by all leaders is required from time to time, such as when implementing unpopular decisions or actions, but the use of coercive power should be kept to the absolute minimum because its overuse only leads to resentment and conflict.

See also

Q1   What is the relationship between leading and managing?

Q5   Can everyone lead?

This is one of the most commonly-asked questions regarding leadership, often depicted as "Are leaders born or made?".

In a general sense, there have been many great individuals throughout history who seem to have been born solely for the purpose of leading. Yes, they learned along the way but it appears that they were put on this earth for a particular purpose. In this regard, we have to say that some extraordinary people were born to lead.

But the focus here is on leadership at a different level, requiring another perspective. Leading others in a work context is not – for the most part – about changing the world, so in an organisational context, it is more accurate to say that leaders are both born and made. The born aspect means that you should really want to lead other people in the first place; it's not everyone's cup of tea and without a strong passion for leading people, it will likely prove more hassle than it is worth. And yes, you do need to possess certain personal characteristics that underpin effective leadership; these are not so easily learned or developed, certainly not in the short term, so some form of foundation is required. The made element is the leadership skills and techniques, such as communication, which can be more readily learned and improved.

Therefore, if you are truly motivated to lead others and have essential qualities in place, it is possible to enhance your leadership potential over time. Of course, some people naturally excel at it over others, but that is the same in every walk of life; we all can learn to ride a bicycle but not all of us can reach the level required to compete in the Tour de France; some leaders just have more of what it takes by nature. But that doesn't mean you cannot build your capacity to lead if you are prepared to work at it.

See also

Q16   What personal attributes are required to be a successful leader?
Q35   What are the core leadership skills that contribute to success?

Q6 Why is having a personal vision so important for leaders?

The notion of having a personal 'vision' can be off-putting for some leaders, particularly those at more junior ranks; it can seem wishy-washy, or beyond the scope of anyone but senior directors. Yet, there is plenty of evidence to demonstrate that a common factor distinguishing the better leaders in organisations, regardless of rank, is the strength of their vision.

A personal vision is a mental picture or broad aim for what you wish to achieve as a leader. For a CEO, this might be building a world-class organisation; for a team leader in Administration, it might be to create a positive working environment where everyone strives to give their best. Your personal vision merely puts into words what should already be in your head; it should define what you want to achieve in your role as a leader over the longer term. Of course, any vision should be challenging, but realistic given the current position of the organisation; unrealistic visions are for dreamers, not leaders.

In any leadership position, a vision is critical for a number of reasons. First, a leader's vision separates them from all other individuals who potentially could hold the post. In fact, you can tell a lot about a leader by the nature of their vision; in essence, it is their calling card. Leaders who lack a vision rarely excel in the role; they tend to be plodders and leaders in name only. Another important reason for having a personal vision is that it can serve as a means of communicating to others, in broad terms, what you want to achieve.

In terms of delivering results, however, your personal vision must serve as the foundation stone for all subsequent actions you take as leader. For a CEO, their personal vision plays an important role in determining the organisational vision. Further down the ranks, a leader's personal vision should be the guiding force behind how they lead. This ability to visualise and articulate a possible future state for an organisation as a whole, or for that part of it for which you are responsible, is a critical success factor. Without a personal vision, your focus is likely to be drawn solely to the

ultimately, the vision is being realised (*How do we know we are getting there?*).

As a leader, your vision sets the ultimate aim; the goals make that more concrete; action is taken to realise those goals; and, finally, progress is measured on an ongoing basis.

Yes, without a vision, you might still make the figures look good, surpass budget year-on-year, or trim costs but that is no unique achievement – there are thousands of leaders out there who can get results. You need to ask yourself what is so special about you, or as was asked in the title of a much-admired leadership book: *Why should anyone follow you?* It is precisely this question that your personal vision seeks to answer.

See also

Q6   Why is having a personal vision so important for leaders?
Q77   Why are organisational vision, mission and values important?
Q78   How should vision, mission and values be developed?
Q79   How should vision, mission and values be used for best effect?

Q8   Why is leading by example so critical?

It should be fairly obvious why leading by example is important. It seems like a question that requires little explanation. Sadly, you only have to look at what has happened in the corporate world in recent years to realise that there is often a major disconnect between what some so-called leaders preach and what they practice. When leaders do not walk-the-walk, it becomes hard for their team-members to take them seriously and, over time, this erodes their credibility. Leaders who continuously fail to set an example are leaders in name only and are forced to adopt aggressive and coercive styles in order to get things done, which only confirms the fact that they are not true leaders in the first place.

Leading by example involves a number of dimensions. Spend some time thinking about your own performance in each of the areas below.

At its very simplest, serving as a role model for others involves setting the right tone in terms of appearance, timekeeping and general work ethic; these are such basic requirements that they are not worthy of detailed attention here. If you fail to get any of these consistently right, the consequences should be pretty clear: you can never lead if you constantly mess up the basics.

On a higher level, leading by example is concerned with two critical areas:

- **Attitude:** As a leader, you always should set the benchmark for the type of attitude you expect others to have at work – being positive and motivated at all times and viewing day-to-day problems as challenges to be overcome. Of course, there always are days when you would rather be somewhere else, but the best leaders can mask these feelings and maintain a positive attitude when they have to. Attitude is infectious.

- **Behaviours:** Equally, you should try always to demonstrate behaviours that you expect to see among your team-members – how you communicate with others, manage your own emotions or cope with difficult situations or people. There is no point in expecting your employees to behave well towards each other, or to your customers, if you spend your days screaming and shouting at work, or acting in ways that create a sense of fear and negativity.

What some leaders seem to forget, or choose to ignore, is that holding any leadership position is akin to being on-stage. People around you notice how you think, act and behave; your shortcomings are magnified under the spotlight. Great leaders remain human at all times, so they suffer from normal personal frailties on occasion, but they find ways to put their best foot forward in terms of their attitude and behaviour most of the time. Yes, they slip up now and again but their general demeanour and overall attitude raises the bar for others. Ask yourself whether you are currently setting a good example?

See also

Q9   Do leaders need to inspire others?
Q11   What do employees look for in a leader?

Q9   Do leaders need to inspire others?

Naturally, leaders need to have some capacity to motivate and inspire others but the notion of the 'inspirational leader' has built up mistakenly to the extent that only those who ooze with charisma are seen as truly effective leaders. Of course, in a work context, this is complete nonsense; many of those who were once deemed to be great business leaders have been shown to have had little other than charisma in terms of talent.

Contrary to the widely-held belief that people are looking for someone to 'follow', when you listen to employees talk about their leaders, you rarely hear them complain because they feel he is not Superman, or that she is not Wonder Woman. Most people have fairly realistic expectations of their leaders and simply want to work for someone who treats them fairly and respects them as individuals. In fact, the majority of employees want a boss who views them as partners in the achievement of goals, not as lemmings willing to follow him / her blindly into the abyss. So, do not get too hung up on the notion of the inspirational leader; instead, focus on how you can bring out the best continuously in those around you in the workplace.

In doing so, accept that some element of charisma is undoubtedly helpful; once it is not mistaken for arrogance and is underpinned by substance too. However, great leaders inspire people in different ways: some through their dedication and hard work, others by the scale of their ideas, or from the genuine concern that they show for people.

If you have charisma, then use it to best effect; otherwise, play to the strengths of your own personality. If you feel that you are not overly-charismatic, do not lose hope, try instead to optimise other strengths to compensate. Maybe you are great at remaining calm in a crisis, or perhaps you can find solutions where others only problems. Each of us has individual talents and a key role of any great leader is to know what they are, so that they play to their own strengths and minimise the impact of their own weaknesses.

- Have you focused only on the job, or did you spend a lot of time trying to manage relationships?
- Did you delay decisions because you were afraid of the reaction you might get, or did you make all your decisions without consultation?
- When did you last say "thank you" to your team? Did they deserve it, or were you just trying to be nice?
- Did you make promises to your people but failed to keep them because you were "too busy"?
- Did you end up staying late to finish-off or improve work that should have been completed by one of your team-members?
- When an unexpected change came up at work, did you think only of the technicalities of implementing that change or did you focus on the impact it might have on your people? Or, was it the reverse, did you spend an inordinate amount of time worrying about how people might react, to the extent that you avoided the change?

These and similar questions can help you to determine your current focus and whether you are too people- or job-orientated at present. Better still, why not discuss the issue individually or collectively with your team, or with someone at work whom you would consider a mentor figure? Ask for feedback on this issue at your next annual appraisal. Whatever options you choose to broaden your self-awareness in this area, you must identify where you currently stand, since you cannot improve if you do not know where improvement is needed.

How you set about addressing any problems you might find in this area depends on any personal shortcomings you identify, but there is plenty of guidance on how to balance common job / people challenges provided throughout **QUICK WIN LEADERSHIP**. In particular, there are two areas where leaders frequently slip up in terms of the job / people dynamic that are worth highlighting:

- **How decisions are made:** Some leaders operate a very 'top-down' approach, whereby they make all the decisions, all of the time. Clearly, there are occasions when decisions are not open to debate, but some degree of consultation is advisable, otherwise employees recognise that their opinions do not count and so they disengage. In contrast, some leaders procrastinate about taking decisions or spend far too much time trying to get everyone on board; this, too, is unhealthy for obvious reasons. When important decisions come up, it is useful to allocate some time for discussion, but also to set a deadline for when the final decision has to be taken, rather than leave it open-ended. By doing this, you impose a discipline on yourself and prevent discussions from dragging on indefinitely.

- **How effective communication is:** The majority of people problems can be traced to some form of communication breakdown. Some leaders do not communicate enough; others engage in too much meaningless communication. The solution here is to define structured daily, weekly and monthly communication events, which should be effectively managed in terms of duration and participation, between you and your team. These are useful, both in giving direction (job) but also in allowing feedback from your team (people).

In reality, there are no hard and fast rules for balancing the needs of the job with those of your people. In most cases, commonsense is all you need.

See also

Q11   What do employees look for in a leader?
Q32   What are the different leadership styles?
Q35   What are the core leadership skills that contribute to success?
Q36   Why is communication so important for leaders?

Q11   What do employees look for in a leader?

Defining what people look for in their leaders at work is not easy, because people naturally look for different things. Yet, there are common needs seen time and time again. In no particular order of importance, and using the terms often used by employees themselves, these common needs include:

- **"To know we matter"**: Employees like to work for someone they respect and who, in turn, respects them. This has many dimensions but, at its simplest level, employees want to be treated as individuals. Most do not want special treatment, just fairness and equality applied to all.

- **"To know where we stand"**: Most people want a leader who acts and behaves in a positive and consistent manner most of the time. Nothing frustrates employees more than someone who has moods, or gives conflicting directions from one day to the next.

- **"To know we can talk to them"**: Employees need to feel that they can talk to their leader – in an appropriate way and at an appropriate time, of course. Many bosses say things like "my door is always open" but that is not much use if people are afraid to go inside. You do not suddenly become approachable as a leader just because you tell people that you are; being seen as someone approachable is the outcome of the total environment that you create, and can only happen if there is a strong connection between you and your team.

- **"To be upfront with us"**: One of the most common expectations voiced by employees is that they want to work for a leader who is honest with them. Of course, you will not be in a position always to give them answers on specific issues – that is just a fact of working life. However, for as much of the time as possible, you should give your people complete and honest answers – they might not like what they hear but, if it is truthful, most of them will respect you for it. For certain, nothing will destroy your credibility with your people faster than being seen to lie to them.

- **"To be upbeat most of the time"**: Frequently, employees express the desire to work for a leader who is 'upbeat' – by that they mean someone who is positive and energetic and brings lots of enthusiasm to the work environment (if only all employees would follow their own advice, but that is not the point here!). 'Dark cloud' leaders just sap the energy and enthusiasm out of others.

- **"To show they care"**: By this, employees usually mean that they want their leader to show concern for them – not in the sense of an agony aunt, but in a way that demonstrates that they are valued members of the team. This means taking a personal interest in them, in their levels of motivation, their development and in creating the best work environment possible.

- **"To have a backbone"**: A strong leader can be direct when necessary, but does so in a firm, non-aggressive manner; with these leaders, people know that there is a line that should not be crossed and they rarely cross it. Strong leaders are comfortable in allowing consultation and involvement because they are confident in handling interactions with their team. By and large, employees hate working for a leader whom they consider weak.

- **"To know what they're at"**: As well as these people-related points, employees also want to work for someone who is good at what they do. A competent leader gives confidence to those around them that they are in control. Employees do not expect you to have all the answers, but they do expect you to have most of them. Equally, when they need guidance, they expect you to be able to provide the necessary support on most occasions.

This is not an exhaustive list, but includes factors high up on most employees' expectations. Your first challenge is to consider how well you currently rate yourself against each of these areas.

Then think of leaders you have worked for in the past whom you admired and list the qualities in them that mattered most to you. Consider how you perform against any additional characteristics you might identify from this exercise.

See also

Q8   Why is leading by example so critical?
Q9   Do leaders need to inspire others?

Q12   Do leaders need to be liked in order to be successful?

This is probably one of the most commonly asked questions and, indeed, concerns about leadership. Most of us want to be liked, at least to some degree, but the desire to be popular often poses significant problems for leaders, particularly those who are just starting out on their leadership career. The simple answer here is that leaders do not need to be liked to be successful; being respected is far more important in terms of achieving results. However, there is nothing simple when it comes to human interactions.

A leader in a work context who is disliked by their team most of the time cannot lead them effectively. As a result, they will be forced to use coercive measures to get things done, which is not leadership at all. Some leaders who fall into this category often think that they are respected, but they mistake respect for fear; the job may get done, but quality and morale suffer. Some 'leaders' even say they do not care what people think of them – sooner or later, they suffer a mighty fall because they have built up so many enemies.

However, leaders who try too hard to be liked by everyone may be popular but are not necessarily respected, because their team-members see them as a pushover. Employees, particularly the stronger or more disruptive characters, can smell such weaknesses and will use it to their advantage.

So, as with many aspects of leadership, it is a matter of balance when it comes to being liked by your team. There has to be some bond between you and your employees, if the relationship is to deliver the optimum results possible. The best leaders intuitively understand that respect is gained by showing their employees that, when need be, they can and will make tough decisions, or act firmly when performance is not up to scratch. However, at other times, they can interact positively with their people or simply have a laugh now and again. As a result, their team-members feel valued, but they also know that they must deliver the expected results.

You must accept that unpopular, but necessary, decisions may lead to short-term disapproval and you must learn to cope with that. However, if you are unpopular more of the time than not, then you are doing something very wrong in terms of being an effective leader.

See also

Q11   What do employees look for in a leader?

Q13 What are the most common mistakes that leaders make?

As each leader is different, and human, they all make mistakes – this is only natural. When a leader learns from a slip-up and gets better as a result, there is a positive outcome. However, some leaders seem to make the same mistakes over and over again. The most common of these include:

- **Suffering from the 'I am the Boss syndrome':** Even today, too many leaders mistakenly believe that, because they are nominated as the leader, others automatically should look up to them, or follow their lead unquestionably. This stems from a fundamental lack of understanding of how employee attitudes to work have changed. People no longer will bow to you just because you are the boss. Employees, at least those who want to hold on to their jobs, will always do the work but the difference between 'job done' and 'job done well' is obvious. You need to see beyond the title and motivate your team continuously towards better performance.

- **Applying the wrong leadership styles:** Leaders need to be flexible today in how they apply their leadership style. Some situations call for a directive approach, whereas others are best addressed by involving employees or including them in the decision-making process. A common mistake for many leaders is not being able to adapt to the different needs of people and situations; they operate from a 'one size fits all' leadership style which, in a modern, complex work environment, does not produce the best results. Without flexibility of approach, a leader will struggle in the role.

- **Lack of focus and follow-through:** Some leaders suffer from a tendency towards a 'flavour of the month' approach, whereby great emphasis is placed on an issue, task or project for a short period of time but then it quickly falls off the agenda. This is not only destructive in terms of achieving results but, when employees learn that their leader does not stick with something, or fails to follow through, they tend to take a wait-and-see approach to all new initiatives. In other words, they will not put in additional effort or take ownership for projects because they know that, if they keep their heads down, sooner or later it will be forgotten about.

- **Lack of feedback:** Most employees want feedback on their performance – if it is presented in a constructive manner. Some leaders fail to provide the necessary feedback on a continuous basis or, when they do, they focus more on the negatives than the positives. The only thing worse for an employee than receiving no feedback at all is hearing more about the one bad thing they did than all the good results they delivered. Sometimes, leaders mistakenly believe that an annual appraisal suffices in terms of feedback, but it does not. If your employees receive both the good and, when deserved, the bad news, then they are likely to try to address their shortcomings. Certainly, they will make more of an effort to improve when they receive rounded feedback than they will if they receive little or none at all, or worse still, get hit by a wave of negativity once every 12 months.

- **Poor communication:** Linked to the above is the fact that some leaders are just poor communicators, perhaps because they do not communicate enough, or they over-rely on static channels such as memos or emails to get their messages out, or they fail to engage employees. Anything you can do as a leader to improve in this area will make a positive and noticeable impact, if sustained over the long term. In doing so, you should focus both on your own skills and on the modes of communication you use.

- **Delegation:** Failings in relation to delegation cover a multitude of sins. Some leaders do not delegate at all and seek to micro-manage to such an extent that they stifle employee enthusiasm and creativity; other leaders believe that they are good delegators, when all they are doing is off-loading mundane work they dislike onto others. When done right, delegation results in a win-win situation for both the leader and the employee. You win in the sense that you free up your time to address other more pressing matters; your employee gains in that the task delegated to them will help them to develop their skills and knowledge in some way.

- **Mishandling change:** Another common failing seen in leaders relates to how they manage change. Some leaders dislike or fear change themselves, so they cling to the *status quo* at all costs; other leaders are 'change junkies', constantly looking for the next big thing, which only lasts until something else replaces it. Even when leaders get the amount of change correct, some mishandle its implementation, which causes other problems. Introducing change must take into account human factors. Some leaders fail to recognise this and seek to drive change through the organisation, without any consultation or explanation, which only leads to resentment and resistance. Others take it too softly-softly, with the result that the change process drags on forever. When it comes to change, clearly define the change and the rationale for it; ensure that the communication process around the change is inclusive and two-way; implement first steps in a timely fashion; quickly identify and address any blockages associated with the implementation; and recognise and reward achievement.

See also

Q32   What are the different leadership styles?
Q35   What are the core leadership skills that contribute to success?
Q36   Why is communication so important for leaders?
Q46   How and when should I delegate?
Q52   How can I motivate and engage my team-members better?
Q98   How should I lead change for best results?

Q14   Why is personal development so necessary for leaders?

Personal development is important for everyone, but it is particularly so for leaders. The complexity of leadership today means that no one individual can have inherently all the talents and skills necessary to excel at all aspects of leading others. Therefore, every leader must update and enhance their skills constantly and work on any identified areas of weakness.

Failing to strive for personal development results in:

- Standing still – and, in an ever-changing business environment, to stand still means to fall behind.

- Fear of high performers around you and particularly those within your own team who show potential – rather than develop such individuals, you will likely do the opposite, holding them back because you fear they will outshine you. In the short term, you lose the motivation and performance benefits of developing these high performers; in the longer term, these individuals move on, where their talents are appreciated more and their career goals nurtured.

- Risk of being unable to sustain your knowledge base, thus limiting your ability to engage in detailed discussions on current or evolving trends, to be creative in how you respond to new problems or simply to project the air of confidence that comes from being informed and up-to-date on work-related matters.

- Narrowing the range of opportunities available to you in your present position – and perhaps damaging your future career prospects, too.

See also

Q15   How can I evaluate how well I am progressing as a leader?
Q16   What personal attributes are required to be a successful leader?

Q15 How can I evaluate how well I am progressing as a leader?

The idea of measuring your own effectiveness as a leader in a formal way might seem like an unnecessary activity; great if you have little else to do, but a luxury when you are busy enough already. Leaders frequently argue that, if people stay, you can assume that they are generally happy with what you are doing. Unfortunately, there are flaws in this thinking.

First, if you want to be the best leader possible, you cannot just accept things as they are; instead, you must aim constantly to enhance all aspects of your skills as a leader. Unless you have some concrete measure of your current strengths and weaknesses, how can you ever hope to improve?

Second, just because your employees stay with you does not signify the absence of problems with your leadership. If there are issues, they will get worse if left unaddressed, so it is better to get them out in the open.

Therefore, you need to measure your leadership effectiveness in a structured way. A self-assessment tool can help you to judge your own effectiveness as a leader, despite the obvious difficulties in being truly objective about your own performance. However, the only true measure of how effective you are as a leader comes from those who are most closely affected by what you do, or do not do – so your superiors and employees must be involved in the measurement process in some way; their feedback is vital.

You can use structured performance appraisals held with employees to gather information about your performance. During these appraisals, which are supposed to be two-way forums in any case, as well as giving feedback to your employees, you also should ask them how they rate your capabilities as a leader. Of course, it takes confidence to ask such questions, but the best leaders recognise the importance of doing so. Appraising your leadership performance in this way will help you to determine how effective you are at delivering on your employees' expectations in terms of how well you lead them. Equally, during your own appraisal with your boss, you should have specific questions in mind for him / her to elicit their views on the quality of your leadership.

Also, most companies now have some form of employee satisfaction survey. If you include appropriate questions, it can provide additional information on how your people collectively view your leadership. This 'snapshot' feedback can give you an indication of potential difficulties, which then can be explored in greater detail through face-to-face discussions with your team.

Measuring your leadership effectiveness need not be an overly complex process but it must provide you with accurate and reliable feedback, which you can act upon to make things better. Without such information, you will not be in a position to focus your personal development efforts.

See also

Q14   Why is personal development so necessary for leaders?
Q19   Why is self-awareness so important for leaders?
Q20   How might I increase my self-awareness?

LEADERSHIP QUALITIES

Q16　What personal attributes are required to be a successful leader?

All leaders require certain skills to be effective. However, though critical, the actual skills of leadership arguably are secondary, because your success as a leader is linked as much to *how you think* and *who you are*, as it is to *what you do*. Certain personal attributes facilitate effective leadership, underpinning the skills and, without strengths in these areas, leadership becomes an uphill struggle regardless of how many skills training courses you attend.

There is no one ideal set of personal qualities. Yet, for leaders to *engage (lead)* and *achieve (manage)*, the characteristics in the diagram below are critical:

These characteristics help you to engage your employees and support you in your efforts to achieve the desired results; they are priority qualities. If you have strengths across these personal characteristics, you are in a better position to apply the skills of leadership, such as communication and leadership style; without these strengths, you will struggle.

This section of **QUICK WIN LEADERSHIP** explores how these key personal characteristics help to make leaders more effective. Before doing so, important questions surrounding how leaders think, and how they improve their understanding of self as a means to building their capabilities, are addressed.

See also

Q14 Why is personal development so necessary for leaders?
Q22 What are the dangers of being too passive or aggressive as a leader?
Q23 Why do leaders need to be passionate and enthusiastic?
Q24 Why is goal-setting so important for leaders?
Q25 Why do leaders need to be self-motivated?
Q26 Why do leaders need high levels of competence?
Q27 Why is empathy important to a leader?
Q28 Why is integrity essential for leaders?
Q29 Why is creativity so vital in a leadership role?
Q35 What are the core leadership skills that contribute to success?
Q84 What is a leadership competence model?
Q100 How might I unify all the principles of leadership?

Q17   What is a leadership mindset?

For the most part, leaders at work are ordinary people who often can do extraordinary things. Of course, they have a range of attributes, skills and expertise that helps them to excel but, at a more fundamental level, all the best leaders are defined by their mindsets.

A common feature of how all great leaders think is that they are deeply motivated towards taking responsibility for others; it is not something they just fall into, or take on board because the pay is better. No, they really do *want* to lead. Without this inner desire, you run the risk of being overwhelmed by the challenges posed by any leadership role.

Another important feature of the leadership mindset is that the best leaders genuinely believe that the route to improved results lies in having highly motivated and engaged employees. They never see employees as a 'means to an end', but rather view them as fundamental to organisational success. And this is more than just words, because their actions every day show it to be something they actually believe in.

In addition, the best leaders:

- Understand that they constantly need to be creative in how they lead others in terms of getting the best out of them, because the tried and tested may not always work.

- Know that telling people what to do all the time might be the easier approach on paper but it is far from the most effective, so they involve their employees in decision-making, where appropriate, and maintain open lines of communication.

- See the individual in each employee and view leading a diverse team as an interesting challenge, not a chore.

- Recognise that holding any leadership position is a privilege and that they have the potential to impact the lives of others in either a positive or negative manner.

These elements of the leadership mindset may seem individually insignificant but, collectively, they provide a clear frame of reference for the best leaders. It is worth spending time reflecting on your own thoughts about leadership because how you act and behave is significantly influenced by how you think.

See also

Q16 What personal attributes are required to be a successful leader?
Q35 What are the core leadership skills that contribute to success?

Q18   How do personal values affect leadership behaviour?

Values are deeply-held beliefs about what is good, bad, appropriate or acceptable, and can be individually unique, or shared by an organisation, community or even a country. Your personal values are deep-rooted in you and have become so throughout a lifetime of experience. Like most people, you may not think too deeply about your own values on a day-to-day basis, but they are there in the background, influencing the choices you make, and, consciously or sub-consciously, they guide how you act and behave, particularly when faced with challenging decisions.

Values-based leadership is about defining the core values that matter to you and using them to guide you in how you lead others. The most admired leaders always identify their deeply-held values and seek to live by them every day, ensuring that these values directly influence their behaviour at work and contribute to all their important decisions and actions.

To strengthen the impact that your values have on how you lead others, the first step is to deepen your understanding of those values. Simply reflecting on what really matters to you in life can help you pinpoint your personal values. Consider:

- Which of your values are non-negotiable?
- How well do you currently live by those values?
- How have you felt in the past if you were forced to compromise them?

Armed with a better understanding of self, you can strive to align what you do on a daily basis more closely to what you believe in.

Unfortunately, life is never all plain sailing and, from time to time, every leader is faced with a moral dilemma in terms of matching their actions as a leader with their fundamental values. On occasion, leaders, often following instructions from above, find themselves forced to walk a tight-rope between what they really believe in and what they are required to do at work. You may have found yourself in similar circumstances in the past, or may do so in the future. There is no simple solution to resolving such dilemmas, as it depends on how strong your values are in the first place, how far you are being asked to compromise them and what the likely consequences of going against them, or not, will be.

However, occasional compromise apart, constantly going against your values is likely to lead to deep unhappiness – and who wants that in life? Equally, if you are working for an organisation where there is constant conflict between your personal values and those of the business, then clearly you are in the wrong place.

See also

Q8   Why is leading by example so critical?
Q9   Do leaders need to inspire others?
Q77   Why are organisational vision, mission and values important?

Q19 Why is self-awareness so important for leaders?

Self-awareness does not always get as much attention in a leadership context as it deserves, but it is an important driver of success for any leader. To put it simply, the best leaders are always highly self-aware and, not only do they know their strengths and weaknesses, but they work hard to address identified shortcomings. As a result, they benefit tangibly in terms of their long-term performance.

But this feature of their make-up also tells us something more fundamental about them. It takes honesty and real courage to acknowledge personal failings, and a lot of self-motivation then to do something about those weaknesses; those who can make that journey possess a strength of character not seen in others who know themselves less well.

Some leaders lack self-awareness; as a result, they continue to act and behave in ways that are counterproductive and, at times, counterintuitive in a leadership role. What they do not seem to realise is that, although they themselves may be oblivious to their own failings, everyone around them is not; this ultimately damages their credibility with their colleagues and employees. This lack of self-awareness may result from many factors, such as arrogance or selfishness, but part of the problem is that some individuals view showing any sign of weakness as something to be avoided, when in reality it should be seen as a positive thing. All of us have individual strengths and weaknesses and there is no shame in admitting that we need help and support in certain areas. In fact, the real shame lies in either failing to accept the weakness in the first place or, worse still, failing to do anything about a known personal shortcoming.

Being conscious of what you are good at, while accepting that you still have plenty to learn, will drive you to constantly raise the personal effectiveness bar. Building your self-awareness can push you to identify where the gaps lie in relation to your ability to lead others; it can also help you to recognise the situations where you excel and those where you perform less strongly. By constantly identifying and addressing your personal areas for improvement, over time you can increase your potential as a leader. You also gain in confidence because you can see how you have learned to translate weaknesses into strengths; and so you become less constrained by your shortcomings.

Leaders who are self aware tend to suffer less from stress and self-doubt. They are comfortable with who they are and, as a result of their strong self-awareness, they also have a greater sense of being in control of their own destinies, which of itself helps to reduce stress.

See also

Q16   What personal attributes are required to be a successful leader?
Q20   How might I increase my self-awareness?
Q30   How might I cope better with stress?

Q20   How might I increase my self-awareness?

Leaders who excel understand the importance of structured and constructive feedback in guiding their efforts to get better at what they do, so they constantly search out opportunities to build their self-awareness.

There are several ways in which you might increase your self-awareness:

- **Self-reflection:** As a starting point, regularly reflect on your own performance by considering objectively how you handled different situations and events.

- **Mentoring:** Find yourself a mentor at work who can give you an independent and experienced view of your performance.

- **Performance appraisals:** 360-degree feedback from peers, superiors, employees and customers gives a very rounded picture of your performance and can highlight areas where you need to improve.

In the absence of a formal appraisal system, you still can solicit feedback from those around you; however, in doing so, you need to consider:

- **Carefully select those from whom you wish to gather feedback:** Make sure they see enough of your day-to-day leadership performance to be able to give you accurate and relevant feedback. At the same time, in making your choices, do not just pick people who simply will tell you what you want to hear.

- **Ask the right questions:** Asking someone "do you think I am a good leader?" is pointless. Break it down into specific areas – for example, communication skills or managing resources and develop relevant questions on each area.

- **Be prepared to listen:** It is natural to challenge points with which we disagree but, in this context, it is best to listen and then probe for understanding once you have heard all the feedback.

- **Accept the points:** If you have chosen carefully the people from whom you gathered feedback, you should accept their comments, particularly if the same points were mentioned by more than one person. Do not develop grudges against people because they told you a few home truths.

Appropriate feedback should help to raise your self-awareness but, unless you take practical steps to address the areas for improvement identified, it all will be a waste of time. Use the simple goal achievement framework described in **Q24**.

See also

Q19 Why is self-awareness so important for leaders?
Q24 Why is goal-setting so important for leaders?
Q48 How might I use mentoring and networking as tools to help me grow as a leader?

Q21 What is the difference between intelligence quotient (IQ) and emotional intelligence (EI)?

In a formal sense, intelligence quotient (IQ) refers to the score achieved on a standardised intelligence test; the concept has been around since the early 1900s. In less formal terms, the term 'IQ' refers to how intelligent we believe a person to be: we say things like, "she has a high IQ", meaning she is fairly smart but in a 'booky' sense. Emotional intelligence (EI) is a more recent concept and describes the ability or capacity of an individual to be aware of, and to manage, their own emotions and those of others. A high EI means that someone is in control of their emotions, strongly self-aware, and can relate and interact well with others.

Every leader needs to be intelligent to some degree, in order to keep up to speed with all the knowledge and technical skills associated with most leadership positions today. But having the highest IQ in the organisation is not necessarily a guarantee of leadership success; people with very high IQ scores tend also to have low emotional intelligence.

EI is clearly critical to the ability to engage with employees. Being on top of your own emotions as a leader means that you can act in a calm, controlled and empathetic manner most of the time; this helps you to apply leadership styles that best respond to any given situation, as opposed to acting on impulse, or letting anger take over. Having a high EI also helps you to relate better with others and, over time, this creates stronger bonds with your team-members.

To succeed in the modern workplace, you need strengths in both IQ and EI, for one without the other creates its own problems. Low IQ can limit you in terms of fundamental aspects of the job, such as decision-making or dealing with financial data. Low EI can make you a nightmare to work for and appear aloof or distant from your employees. As part of your efforts to develop your self-awareness, you should search for opportunities that would help you to measure both your IQ and EI.

See also

Q19   Why is self-awareness so important for leaders?

Q22   What are the dangers of being too passive or aggressive as a leader?

One of the more important qualities for a leader is the ability to maintain high levels of self-control. Work-life, with its multitude of stressful situations, has the potential to test every leader to the limit. But the best leaders can respond, most of the time, in a calm and controlled manner no matter what they are faced with. In other words, they are assertive individuals.

If you currently lack self-control as a leader, then other people and situations control the way you behave and you are shackled in your ability to lead. Being in control of your emotions is not about hiding all your natural impulses; that is neither possible, nor welcome. It does mean, however, that you recognise the triggers that unbalance you and, over time, learn to minimise the effect they have on how you react.

Even great leaders lose their temper now and again; but only infrequently, and mostly because they decide to do so, not out of uncontrolled impulses. Being aggressive most of the time is an entirely different proposition and, for leaders who are aggressive by nature, it causes them significant problems; if you regularly lose your cool, you are simply less effective. Constant aggressive responses mean that you become like a walking time-bomb to those around you, creating an atmosphere of fear and anxiety, which has obvious repercussions. In addition, by behaving so, you eventually create an environment at work where other people, usually the stronger characters in the team, believe that they need to be aggressive in response and life quickly becomes a constant battle with them. Those who do not like being in such an atmosphere, usually the smarter ones, will leave, damaging your team. Constant, aggressive behaviour is self-defeating and always does more harm than good.

On the other hand, being too passive – where you are seen as a pushover by your employees – also damages your ability to lead. Shying away from difficult situations and people, or avoiding conflict simply because you are afraid of it, means that you cannot lead effectively. The long-term consequences of being too passive are that your team-members, again particularly the stronger ones, sense that it is they who are ultimately in control and will use that knowledge to their advantage.

Assertiveness essentially is about controlling your responses to any given individual or situation and finding the right balance between aggressive and passive impulses. At times, this may mean being very firm and direct with people but doing so in a way where you are not screaming and shouting or acting irrationally. Equally, admittedly on rare occasions, being a little passive might be the best route, whereby you ignore or avoid conflict simply because it would be of little value to pursue it.

As human beings, we are a mix of aggressive and passive behaviours. Some situations can bring out aggression in certain leaders – for example, when dealing with a subordinate – whereas others – dealing with the boss – bring out a degree of passivity. The problem with too much passiveness or aggression is that, in either case, you are not really in control and, when control decreases, the ability to remain rational also declines. Being assertive allows you to stay rational, not emotional, and this helps you lead more effectively.

If you currently find yourself operating in passive or aggressive mode for much of the time, you need to change this if you want to improve as a leader. A good first step is to think about your predominant behaviours currently: are they aggressive, passive or are you already assertive most of the time? Then think about how you can fix the problem. Many of the other questions in **QUICK WIN LEADERSHIP** will give you guidance on various aspects of leadership behaviour which, if followed, can combine to make you more assertive over time.

See also

Q16   What personal attributes are required to be a successful leader?
Q35   What are the core leadership skills that contribute to success?

Q23   Why do leaders need to be passionate and enthusiastic?

Emotions are infectious and leaders play an important role in setting the general climate and tone at work. When a leader is passionate and enthusiastic, this creates a generally positive working environment; the best leaders have high energy levels, which makes people feel good about being around them. Of course, the reverse is true and prolonged negativity from a leader ultimately depresses everyone.

Effective leaders have an ability to remain upbeat most of the time because they really do enjoy the leadership role. They recognise that, if they do not project an air of passion and enthusiasm, then the team and, ultimately, the results will suffer. You cannot fake positive emotions such as these over the long-term; unless they are genuine, people quickly see through them.

Better leaders get through the normal short-term lows in life without allowing them impact too negatively on how they act and behave at work. They make a conscious, if difficult, effort to remain relatively upbeat, even when they do not feel up to doing so. Of course, they may dip somewhat from time to time but not to the extent that they damage the atmosphere at work. When there are wider, more substantial issues affecting their motivation – be they work or non-work related – those who excel in leadership roles take pro-active steps to resolve those difficulties because they recognise that, unless they do so, their levels of enthusiasm and positive attitude will be damaged.

To reflect on this important area, consider the following questions:

- Are you really enthusiastic about leading others, or was it the extra money that attracted you to the role?
- Did you actively seek to become a leader or were you just next in line?
- Do you really believe in the company that you are working for?
- Do you get a real buzz out of what you do every day?

- Do you consider dealing with people problems at work to be a challenge or a chore?

- Do you take personal satisfaction when your team performs well?

- Are there issues at work that impact negatively on your levels of enthusiasm? What have you done, or could you do, to remove these blockages?

- Can you leave problems behind at work at the end of the day or do you dwell on them constantly?

- When you wake up every day, do you feel good about going to work or do you have to drag yourself there?

- Are you happy generally with your life?

- Would you describe yourself as being relatively fit and healthy?

- Do you take pro-active steps to address the non work-related problems you face or do you let them fester and get you down?

These, and other similar questions, are vital considerations for you because they impact deeply on your ability to be passionate and enthusiastic in the leadership role.

See also

Q16   What personal attributes are required to be a successful leader?
Q35   What are the core leadership skills that contribute to success?

Q24   Why is goal-setting so important for leaders?

Goals are good, with one prerequisite: they must be realistic and achievable. Unfortunately, some people set unrealistic goals for themselves, given their talent or their willingness to put the required effort into realising them. Avoid falling into this trap. All great leaders are goal-orientated and excel at setting personal and work-related goals; they also make sure that, not only are those goals grounded in reality, but that clear plans are put in place to realise them.

A common denominator seen in all successful leaders is that they set sensible personal goals, which serve to challenge them, for sure, but are within their potential to achieve. They also know that just setting goals is only a first step; achieving them requires them to be both *efficient* and *effective* in moving towards them.

In setting your own personal goals, it is important to recognise that efficiency and effectiveness are not the same thing:

- **Efficiency** comes from having an approach to planning, such as a diary r Blackberry, which you use daily; using such tools provides structure to your day and allows you to prioritise activities on an ongoing basis.

- **Effectiveness** is a different matter entirely and involves setting goals and working back from them to determine what needs to be done to realise them.

To be really effective, you need to follow a few simple steps:

Making Personal Goals Materialise		
Step 1	Define your goal	Begin by defining your **goal** as clearly as possible. Be as specific as you can.
Step 2	Identify key activities	List the key **activities** required to achieve that goal. Do not, at this stage, think about when these will be done – just focus on the broad activities that must happen to make this goal a reality.

Making Personal Goals Materialise		
Step 3	Break activities into tasks	Then, break these broader activities into more specific **tasks** that need to be carried out within that activity.
Step 4	Sequence the tasks	Now, think about whether certain tasks need to be carried out before others? Put the tasks into some form of logical sequence. This will help with deciding deadlines, etc.
Step 5	Develop timelines	For each of the tasks that you identify, define **timelines** for when you would like to implement them, with a clear finish date. Depending on the goal in question, timelines might be quite specific or could be structured on a short, medium and long term basis.
Step 6	Use a scheduling tool	Use your current **scheduling tool** to plan these tasks, including start and finish dates as appropriate.
Step 7	Monitor progress	**Monitor progress** at frequent and regular intervals so that any 'drift' can be identified early.

This structured approach, with set timelines, will make you both efficient and effective in setting and realising your goals.

In a work context, you can apply the same principles to collective goal-setting because it is just as important to have a clear view of what you are trying to achieve for your organisation, or that part of it for which you are responsible. To do this, you should work with your team, where possible, to define tangible and meaningful goals that serve to guide your efforts. Then, define all the tasks and activities that need to happen in order to make those goals a reality, agreeing timeframes, responsibilities and completion schedules. From that, you need to ensure that the work happens within the agreed deadline and to the standard required. You can review progress towards the goals through weekly and monthly meetings.

Once work-related goals are set, pay attention to building and sustaining 'buy-in' for them, motivating others and recognising achievement along the way. If you do this well, you will be surprised at how your employees come to see the goals as being their own; with the result that those who work for you tend to feel part of something bigger than themselves. Of course, when collective goals are achieved, you should always recognise and reward performance across the team.

You also can apply these principles of personal and collective goal-setting when you are helping individual team-members to set their personal goals for a forthcoming period as part of annual appraisals. It is a very simple framework – which makes it attractive – but more importantly, it works.

See also

Q16 What personal attributes are required to be a successful leader?
Q35 What are the core leadership skills that contribute to success?

Q25   Why do leaders need to be self-motivated?

Many people say they want to achieve certain things, but wanting and doing are two different states entirely. One of the distinguishing features of a great leader is their high levels of self-motivation; they constantly push themselves for greater achievement. This trait can help them to pro-actively confront difficult situations and gives others a sense of confidence and comfort; this drive and determination helps them to get better results.

There is no magic solution to self-motivation but here are some basic tips that can help you:

- **Set personal and work goals:** Do not just set goals – write them down and display them prominently where they will serve as a reminder. Tell others too about your goals and get them to follow up with you at periodic intervals.

- **Stick to your plan:** When you make plans to help you realise your goals, stick to them rigidly. One of the most deflating things you can do is to procrastinate; missing a deadline can be upsetting and, in turn, this can cause you to throw in the towel, while hitting an agreed deadline can have the opposite effect.

- **Recognise your achievements:** When you achieve a goal, or even an important milestone on the way, make sure you treat yourself, or if it is a team-related issue, recognise their efforts.

- **Always focus on the positives:** This is always easier said than done, of course, but dwelling on negatives can stymie your self-motivation.

- **Stay fit and healthy:** Maintaining high levels of self-motivation is hard when you lack drive and energy. It is always easier to face life's challenges when you feel in good shape.

See also

Q16   What personal attributes are required to be a successful leader?
Q35   What are the core leadership skills that contribute to success?

Q26 Why do leaders need high levels of competence?

On one level, the reasons why a leader needs to be competent on work matters are obvious. As the head of the team, you are constantly expected to give direction and, for this, you need to have the right competences. Becoming a better leader does not require you to be an expert in all fields, but you do need to broadly understand the various jobs that the individuals who report to you undertake, so that you can accurately guide them when required. Competence, in effect, is a mix between knowledge and skills.

When you have the required knowledge, you feel more confident and in control of given situations and, in turn, this will have implications for how you behave. This is often overlooked by leaders, so make sure you keep yourself up-to-date continuously with knowledge relevant to your role. The extent of your knowledge also impacts on your capacity to analyse and solve problems and to find creative solutions.

As well as being knowledgeable, all leaders must possess a wide range of skills. The variety of the job- and people-related skills required to be effective as a leader over a career can be quite daunting; as can the fact that they change with progression. For example, the technical skills required at a supervisory level become less relevant when you reach the position of head of department and new job-related skills kick in.

Can any one individual hope to master all of the skills required at all times? Of course not, and unfortunately some leaders do not even try to develop their potential, but you should always view leadership as a journey and not a destination and never stop learning new things.

As a personal exercise:

- List five areas where you have expanded your knowledge-base substantially in the past year.
- Identify five new job- or people-related skills that you have newly learned or further enhanced over the past year.

A blank answer page here should set alarm bells ringing.

See also

Q16   What personal attributes are required to be a successful leader?
Q35   What are the core leadership skills that contribute to success?

Q27   Why is empathy important to a leader?

Empathy, defined as having some understanding of, and being sensitive to, the feelings and thoughts of others, is a vital quality for any leader. It contributes to overall emotional intelligence and impacts on a leader's ability to build and sustain relationships with others. Bob Galvin, former CEO of Motorola, captured the essence of empathy when referring to his father, the founder of the company:

> *"Dad once looked down at the assembly line of women and thought, 'These are all like my own mom – they have kids, homes to take care of, people who need them'. It motivated him to work hard because he saw his own mom in all of them. That's how it all begins – with respect and empathy."*

Having an ability to empathise with others not only allows a leader to build stronger and more meaningful bonds with people, but it also helps them to determine what style of leadership works best in any given situation. By being closely in tune with human nature, empathetic leaders also have a natural tendency towards building positive relationships with their team-members; they are more likely to show a real concern for their levels of motivation, monitor it, notice if it is out of sync, find out why and deal with any blockages. Having said that, being empathetic does not make them a soft touch, or turn them into a mother-hen; their ability to read people also helps them to spot quickly when someone is trying to pull the wool over their eyes.

One mistake that some leaders make is that they expect everyone to act and think in similar ways. But this can never happen, for people are all different and particularly so as the workplace becomes more diverse. Being able to see things from the perspective of others is critical for leaders today and you can only truly excel at relationship-building if you can put yourself in the shoes of others. Unfortunately, becoming more empathetic is not something you can hope to achieve overnight, for it is one of those personal qualities that, at best, takes time to develop; some would argue that you either have it or you do not. However, for all the complexity of human nature, you do not need to be a psychologist either to understand that the common expectations of employees include wanting to be valued and respected by their leader; so in that sense, even the most unempathetic person can tune in to others at a surface level at least.

See also

Q16　What personal attributes are required to be a successful leader?
Q35　What are the core leadership skills that contribute to success?

Q28 Why is integrity essential for leaders?

Having high levels of integrity has always been important for leaders but, given all that has occurred in the business world in recent times, it is becoming more of a demand than an expectation for many employees. It should come as no surprise that people do not like being lied to, or fobbed-off with half-truths; your employees expect honesty and integrity. Maintaining strong integrity should be a core priority for you, if you want to retain credibility amongst your peers and employees.

Important steps in this regard include:

- Be true to your word. Tell the truth and abide by your commitments.
- Define your values and principles and stick to them.
- Never blatantly lie to your people.
- Always strive to do the right thing.
- Never steal the ideas of others or take credit for someone else's efforts.
- Recognise that telling people you will get back to them but never doing so is a form of lying.
- Understand that saying "I don't know the answer" is not, in moderation, a weakness for a leader and is far more acceptable than bluffing.

Very few individuals ever admit to lacking integrity and most leaders place it high on their list of priorities. However, it is important to be realistic too and recognise that integrity poses challenges, which often get ignored in theoretical discussions on the subject, but are a fact of daily life for leaders in organisations. There are some occasions where you cannot be as open and honest with your employees as perhaps you might like to be; from time to time, you may not be in a position to give your employees the full picture on a particular issue, or you may be forced to withhold information that will have an impact on them. Does this mean that you do not have integrity? Hardly, these situations are a reality for leaders. But it is the degree of the problem which is of concern here. If you are constantly faced with situations where you have to keep your people in the dark, or regularly feed them misleading information, then this should pose questions for you on the issue of integrity.

Integrity, at a deeper level, means more than just telling the truth. It relates to living by your personal values. It means striving to make the right choice, even when another alternative might prove more advantageous for you personally. In addition, those who have integrity are forthright with others, never operating under the radar or behind the scenes. When they have a problem, either with an individual or regarding a decision or policy, they confront it openly, applying assertive behaviours, of course.

Again, the workplace, with its potential for political games and competition for attention, can present any leader with difficult choices from time to time. Striving to remain aloof from the 'game' in order to retain total integrity may be the idealistic choice but, in reality, it can close doors to your ambitions. Such dilemmas reinforce the need to have personal values to guide you and, while some compromise is always unavoidable, the extent of those concessions depends upon what you personally can live with.

However, despite the practical challenges surrounding integrity, always remember one fact: if you lose your integrity, you have little else left.

See also

Q16   What personal attributes are required to be a successful leader?
Q35   What are the core leadership skills that contribute to success?

Q29   Why is creativity so vital in a leadership role?

Creativity has grown in importance for leaders in recent years. As organisational life has increased in complexity, tried and tested approaches no longer fit the bill, so the need to search for creative and innovative solutions is greater now than ever before. Factors driving this need to be more innovative include:

- Advances in technology.
- Changing business climate.
- Growing customer expectations and demands.
- Increased competition.
- Greater need for competitiveness.

Faced with the pressure to deliver continuous improvement, the ability to be creative or, at the very least, to be able to design and manage processes that encourage innovation, helps leaders to deliver improved organisational performance as a whole, or within that part of the business that falls under their remit.

You are faced with a number of challenges in this regard:

- **Make the most of your own creative skills:** Some people are more naturally creative than others, but everyone has the ability to come up with new ideas, if we allow ourselves the time and space for reflection and thought. As a leader, you are constantly busy, and sometimes the day-to-day demands can take over, leaving you with little time to stand back and explore more innovative ways of doing things. Regardless of how creative you believe yourself to be, it is critical that you allow time for *thinking* as well as *doing*. By taking time to examine trends, to visit best-in-class organisations, to think about how things might be done differently, you are as capable as anyone else of being creative.

- **Create an environment that harnesses the creativity of others:** Creativity does not just happen magically within an organisation. You must create an overall environment where not only is innovation seen as a priority for everyone, but which encourages employees to continuously propose ideas and solutions. Often employees have good ideas about where improvements can be made, but sometimes either the culture prevents them from expressing these ideas, or there are no structured platforms for them to do so. It is critical that you ensure that any such blockages to creativity are removed, and that employees come to view making suggestions as being an integral part of their role, not something separate from it, or an activity to be done only occasionally.

By making the most of your own creative talents and through harnessing the creativity of others, you can make a big difference, over time, not only in terms of how the work is organised and structured, but with regard to the quality of the outcomes too. By involving others in that effort, you bind your team more closely together and create common goals and increased involvement. In doing so, you often can identify those who lack commitment or motivation, because that will show in their lack of interest in, or unwillingness to seek and find new ideas. This, of itself, is useful information for any leader.

See also

Q16   What personal attributes are required to be a successful leader?
Q35   What are the core leadership skills that contribute to success?

Q30   How might I cope better with stress?

Stress is much talked about in modern work life but extremely hard to define. It can have different consequences, depending upon the individual, and personal thresholds in terms of coping with it vary widely. What one person views as a stressful situation may be seen as part of the 'buzz' to another. However, there are clearly potential downsides, both physical and psychological, associated with too much stress.

Leaders are particularly susceptible to stress as a result of the pressures they face on a daily basis; in fact, some argue that being in a leadership position significantly increases the risk level. The first difficulty for any leader is to recognise when stress shifts from being a positive to a negative force; often, you are the last one to know if you are suffering from it. That is why it is important to listen to colleagues, employees, friends and, most importantly, family members. They often can see what we fail, or refuse, to see.

In seeking to cope with stress, recognise that, just as it affects people in different ways and to differing degrees, how you best cope with it will be largely personal in nature and as such, it is really only possible to provide a menu of Dos and Don'ts in terms of coping with stress. Only you can decide which are of interest or useful to you:

Do	Do not
• Monitor your own stress levels, but also ask and listen to others whom you know and trust.	• Confuse harmful stress with the normal feelings of being under pressure from time to time.
• Accept when others tell you that there are noticeable symptoms that you are likely suffering from stress.	• Allow yourself to become stressed about situations over which you have no control.
• Try to identify the source of the stress. Can the source be removed or avoided and, if not, can you find ways of coping better with it?	• Ignore prolonged symptoms that deep down you know are unusual, such as constant fatigue, mood swings or chest pains.
• Consider how you can change your reactions to the source of the stress, if it cannot be avoided.	• Make the mistake that you can battle your way through the problem indefinitely without potentially causing lasting damage
• Talk to your superiors about how you are feeling – don't make the mistake that this is a sign of weaknesses. Be assertive; particularly if you are feeling overworked or bullied, deal with it.	• Use drugs or alcohol as a release mechanism for coping with stress.
• Make time for relaxation – take regular exercise, maintain a balanced diet and do things you enjoy doing.	• Withdraw from family and social networks by internalising your feelings.
• Seek help and advice.	• Take your stress out on those close to you.

See also

Q16   What personal attributes are required to be a successful leader?

Q35   What are the core leadership skills that contribute to success?

LEADERSHIP
SKILLS

Q31   What are the main theories of leadership?

To provide a context for the key skills highlighted later, it is useful first to look briefly at some main theories and styles of leadership which will be the focus of the first few questions in this section.

As with all aspects of management thinking, leadership theory continues to evolve in response to changing social and work dynamics. A review of the development of leadership theory shows that there has been a gradual shift away from the belief that leadership is an inherent ability, reserved only for the select few, to an activity within the reach of many.

The most well-known leadership theories include:

- **Great Man and Trait theories:** The earliest theories of leadership focused on the notion that leaders were born not made; given the prevailing attitudes at the time, leadership also was seen as being primarily within the domain of men, hence the 'Great Man' concept. These theories either asserted that an individual was born to be an outstanding leader, or that they had to possess specific inherent qualities associated with effective leadership.

- **Behavioural theories:** These theories generally took the opposite view about leadership, in that they argued that leaders were made, not born. The focus here was on what leaders do, rather than who they were, and the case was made that success as a leader resulted from definable behaviours that could be learned.

- **Contingency / Situational theories:** These theories broadly argue that leadership effectiveness is based on responding to particular variables or situations and, as such, no one approach to leadership is effective in all cases. Contingency theory thus defined leadership style, ranging from task-orientation at one end to relationship-orientation at the other. Situational leadership focused on the behaviours that leaders should apply in response to given situations.

- **Participative theories:** Participative leadership theories promote the idea that the best leadership approach is one that takes the ideas and contributions of team-members into account.

- **Transactional theories:** These theories are based on the narrow belief that individuals are best led through a system of rewards and punishment, with full authority for how the work is to be done remaining with the leader. The transactional leader views leading others as a form of transaction, whereby rewards are given for good performance and punishment meted out for underperformance.

- **Transformational theories:** Transformational leadership is an approach to leading others whereby the leader motivates and inspires others through developing a compelling vision, their charismatic nature and their enthusiasm for the role, delivering positive results both for the organisation and those working within it.

All these theories have contributed in some way to current leadership thinking; modern approaches to leadership essentially are a combination of many of them:

- The present focus on the attributes needed by leaders has its roots in the trait theories.

- The belief that a leader must have the ability to adapt their approach to different people and situations can be traced to contingency and situational leadership models.

- The promotion of the need for greater inclusivity, working closely with employees, relates back to the participative theories.

- The notion of a leader establishing a clear vision and having some ability to inspire others is linked to transformational leadership and even the idea that leaders cannot ignore underperformance, and rightly so, has undertones of transactional leadership.

See also

Q32   What are the different leadership styles?
Q100 How might I unify all the principles of leadership?

Q32   What are the different leadership styles?

There are as many models that seek to describe the various leadership styles as there are theories of leadership, ranging from the simple to the complex. But, keeping things straightforward, your challenge as a leader is essentially two-fold:

- **Achieve:** In terms of getting the results you want, you must decide how much *direction* to give your team, or individuals within it and how much *control* you must exercise over their actions.

- **Engage:** In relation to the engaging with them, you will have to consider how much to *involve* them in the decision-making process and how much *autonomy* or freedom to give them in the completion of their duties.

Obviously, if you exercise high levels of *direction* and *control*, you reduce the *involvement* and *autonomy* of your employees, so it is always a juggling act and the specific approach you take will be influenced by many factors.

Using these four elements – direction, control, involvement and autonomy – a simple model of leadership styles can be developed:

These are not rigid styles that you jump in and out of, but rather a form of continuum across which you smoothly move back and forth depending upon what is required. Notice also that there is another dimension that impacts on the leadership style you adopt, namely the levels of trust and respect between you and your team. As trust and respect grows, the nature of your approach should naturally change.

The three broad styles in the model can be described as follows:

- **Steering style:** This indicates that you take a direct and active role in guiding the actions of your team, or individual members within it. In doing so, you seek to exercise high direction and control over what they do, which naturally means they have low levels of involvement and autonomy at that time. In applying this style of leadership, it is important that you do not confuse it with being aggressive, because aggression is not a style of leadership in any case, nor does it deliver the best results over the long term. However, you may be firm and assertive if that is what is required. The steering style essentially means that you are more achievement-focused (getting things done) and less concerned with the needs of the team at that particular point in time; you steer their actions in the direction you want them to go, because that is what is called for. It is an essential style, where decisions have to be made quickly, or where a change has to be implemented that is beyond your control and not open to debate. It could also be the approach adopted when a team-member steps out of line. There are many occasions when you may apply this style and, once it is not accompanied by aggressive behaviours, it is perfectly acceptable.

- **Engaging style:** Here you loosen the reins a little and increase the involvement and / or autonomy of your team because you feel that is what is called for. This may mean including them in the decision-making process, or allowing them to propose solutions to given problems. It might involve different levels of engagement: for example, on some occasions, it might simply involve explaining decisions already made to your team – you may not be in a position or willing to alter the decision, but at least you are prepared to listen to their concerns; on other occasions, you consult with your team about decisions to be made, or allow them relatively high levels of autonomy in their actions. You always remain in control, but you are more people-focused using this style. This style is beneficial when you want to harness the input of your team, or particular individuals within it, and can be great for problem-solving and decision-making.

- **Facilitating style:** This involves allowing the team or particular individuals very high levels of involvement and autonomy of action. In some ways, as the leader, you are almost defunct because the team is essentially self-managing; clearly, this is a style you could only ever use if you had a very high-performing team where there was strong mutual trust and respect. Using this style, you might define a problem for the team, explain broadly the outcome you expect but let them decide how to devise and implement a solution. You know from experience that they are capable of making the right decisions and that, should problems arise, they will come to you for guidance.

In seeking to determine which style you should use, there is no step-by-step framework to guide you; a lot simply comes from experience. However, in any given day, you should be using a mix of styles – certainly, Steering and Engaging – depending upon the situation or people involved. Having the ability to apply the 'right' leadership style is another example of how leaders need to think as well as do.

See also

Q33 What influences the style of leadership adopted by a leader?
Q84 What is a leadership competence model?
Q100 How might I unify all the principles of leadership?

Q33 What influences the style of leadership adopted by a leader?

The three identified styles – steering, engaging and facilitating – are straightforward in principle, but it is never as easy to apply the styles in practice. So many factors have an influence on the approaches you adopt that it is impossible to provide guidance on every potential scenario that might arise. However, in deciding which styles to use on any given occasion, there are a number of common influences to consider:

- **Personal capabilities and preferences:** Obviously, to be flexible in your approach requires particular attributes and skills on your behalf and, in particular, the ability to read situations, judge people, communicate effectively and remain calm and in control. Without these qualities and talents, you will find it difficult to shift smoothly from one style to another. Equally, it is through personal preference that you decide which style or styles you wish to apply; some people are more comfortable maintaining high levels of control all the time, whereas others like to involve their people.

- **Team effectiveness:** Where your team lies in terms of its overall effectiveness plays an important role in influencing the predominant style you adopt with them as a unit. If your team is well-established and performing well, you are more likely to apply engaging or facilitating styles more often, because you know the team are ready for this. On the other hand, for new teams, or when you take over an existing team for the first time, you must use the steering style initially until you establish yourself among them and get them operating to a high level. Over time, as the team develops in the way that you want, you can move towards engaging or facilitating styles.

- **Individual performance:** Different team-members perform at varying levels and even good team-members can have low points; you always must adjust your style in response. This change is subtle but, as a rule, higher-performing team-members warrant less direction and control than poor performers and require the application of engaging or facilitating styles more frequently. Equally, a new team-member who is still learning the ropes naturally requires more direction and control than someone who has been doing the job for a long time and thus requires you to use the steering style.

- **Situations:** Different situations require the application of different styles. For example, when time deadlines are tight, you may have to use the steering style to ensure outcomes are met, whereas if changes are required to work practices, this may allow for greater involvement of your team in the decision-making process and so the engaging or facilitating styles are more appropriate .

The ability to develop the required level of flexibility makes the application of leadership style a skill that takes time to develop and improve. Like any skill, you get better at it with practice, if you do the right things of course. All leaders say they are committed to flexibility but not all have the capacity to do so to the extent required in the modern workplace.

See also

Q16   What personal attributes are required to be a successful leader?
Q32   What are the different leadership styles?
Q34   How can a leader be flexible and adaptive without seeming inconsistent?
Q49   What makes an effective team?

Q34   How can a leader be flexible and adaptive without seeming inconsistent?

A major concern for all leaders, when talking about flexibility in styles, is that, by being flexible, they might be seen as somehow inconsistent. This is a valid concern and, as such, requires you to consider how and when you apply the various styles.

How to apply the leadership styles
This relates to the behaviours you use when applying a particular style. If, for example, you are the type of leader who is nice to some individuals, but nasty to others, then clearly you easily stand accused of being inconsistent, and indeed unfair. Or, if you were calm in one situation, but went berserk in another, then that would not win you any favours either in the consistency stakes. However, in applying leadership styles, there is no such danger, if you adhere to some basic principles:

- **Assertiveness:** No matter with whom they are dealing, or what situation they are facing, the best leaders remain calm and in control of their emotions most of the time. Their tone of voice and body language when dealing with a difficult employee (steering) is not radically different from when they are consulting the most positive member of the team (engaging). If you have a calm demeanour in all situations, you are unlikely to be accused of inconsistency.

- **Fairness:** In all their dealings with employees, better leaders also adhere to the basic rules of fairness. You should never fall into the trap of showing favouritism to one team-member over another in terms of how you treat or interact with them.

When to apply the leadership styles
It is vital that you remain consistent in when you apply the various leadership styles. As you use a particular style in a given situation, with the team as a whole, or with specific individuals, you become better at

recognising which approach works best. Why then would you take a different approach when faced with a similar scenario in future?

Accusations of inconsistency usually stem not from *what* you do but *how* you do it. By adopting an assertive behaviour model for all your interactions, you are unlikely to fall foul of this issue.

If and when it does arise, even if it is an unfair accusation, you should always listen to the accuser and explain why you took the approach you did as opposed to the approach they may have wanted you to take.

See also

Q32 What are the different leadership styles?
Q33 What influences the style of leadership adopted by a leader?

Q35 What are the core leadership skills that contribute to success?

The array of skills necessary to succeed as a leader is broad. In fact, almost any skill you possess is likely to help you in some way as you fulfil your diverse functions. Of course, skills gaps quickly become a major liability too; out there in the spotlight of leadership, failings are magnified. And so all leaders constantly must work hard to enhance their skills.

In particular, a leader requires strengths across four skill-sets critical to their overall levels of effectiveness, as these skills help them to both lead and manage:

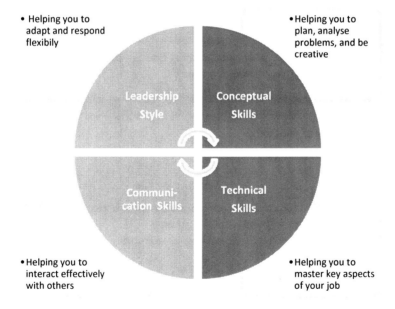

- Helping you to adapt and respond flexibily

- Helping you to plan, analyse problems, and be creative

Leadership Style

Conceptual Skills

Communication Skills

Technical Skills

- Helping you to interact effectively with others

- Helping you to master key aspects of your job

It would be wrong to suggest that every successful leader is a master of all these four skill-sets but they do have talents in all of the following areas:

- **Conceptual:** These skills help a leader to see the 'big picture' and ensure that the organisation, or that part of it for which they are responsible, is consistently in tune with a changing operating environment. The best leaders are good at assimilating information, analysing complex issues, problem-solving and decision-making.

- **Technical:** All leaders must handle the range of technical skills associated with a leadership role competently. At junior levels, these skills may relate directly to the work undertaken, or those that facilitate the workload, such as preparing rosters, for example; as the leader progresses, they may assume greater responsibility for other technical skills, such as planning and financial management.

- **Communication:** All leaders need to communicate effectively, so that they connect with others; this means being able to interact well with colleagues, superiors, customers and employees.

- **Leadership style:** Every leader needs to improve their ability to adjust how they deal with, and respond to, the roller-coaster ride that is life in organisations today.

As an exercise, consider what strengths you have in each of these skill-sets and, more importantly from a development point of view, define areas of improvement for yourself.

See also

Q16   What personal attributes are required to be a successful leader?
Q32   What are the different leadership styles?
Q100   How might I unify all the principles of leadership?

Q36 Why is communication so important for leaders?

There are few certainties when it comes to leadership, but it is no exaggeration to say that you cannot be an effective leader unless your communications skills are highly developed. The ability to communicate well with others impinges on everything you do as a leader; whether through face-to-face or written channels, you are always communicating and the amount of time you spend doing so simply reinforces its importance.

For example, you need to communicate effectively to:

- Maintain positive relationships with others.
- Provide direction for the organisation, or that part of it for which you are responsible.
- Build and sustain high-performing teams.
- Motivate and inspire others.
- Handle conflict.
- Manage change.
- Provide feedback.
- Recruit new team-members.

And the list goes on. In fact, unless you sit in a darkened room all day, you are constantly communicating, so a failure to do it well has major implications on your ability to lead. In exploring the importance of communication for you as a leader, you should reflect on both your own talents in this area and the structures and channels you have in place to facilitate communication.

Personal skills
Striving to build your personal communication skills constantly should be a top priority. To give yourself a sense of where you currently stand in this critical area, consider the following questions:

- How well do you understand the dynamics of communication and, in particular, the importance of tone and body language?
- When communication breaks down at work, do you have a tendency to blame others for it, or do you reflect on your own contributions to the problem?
- When was the last time you had formal communication training? What did you change / improve as a result of that training?
- What do you think your superiors, colleagues and employees might say about you as a communicator, if asked?
- Do you avoid certain communication situations because you lack the confidence to maintain control?
- How do your emotions currently affect the way you communicate? Are you good at staying calm or have you a tendency to fly off the handle?
- Are you more comfortable writing an email / memo to convey an important topic, where you have time to gather your thoughts, review drafts and be confident that you have sent the best version of the message?
- Are you more comfortable communicating in person, where you can spontaneously discuss the matter in an interactive way?
- Do you over-rely on one particular channel of communication?
- Are you better at communicating up or down the chain of command?
- Do you feel confident when you communicate face-to-face with others?
- How productive are the briefings and meetings that you hold? Are they well-controlled, whilst at the same time giving everyone a chance to contribute? How well do you deal with difficult participants?

After reflecting on these questions, think about your areas for improvement as a communicator and identify concrete action you can take in the coming weeks and months to build your capabilities.

Structures and channels

In reviewing your effectiveness as a communicator, look beyond your own skills to wider issues such as the effectiveness of the structures and channels currently in place that facilitate internal communication within your team, and with other parts of the organisation.

Useful questions in this regard include:

- Who are the internal stakeholders that you interact with most frequently at work (for example, employees, superiors, colleagues, etc.)?

- What are the key messages that you need to convey to each of these stakeholders?

- How often is formal communication required in order to get those messages across?

- What structures / channels are in place to reach each key stakeholder group?

- How well do these structures / channels work at present? Where are the gaps?

- What concrete action might you take to address those gaps?

These questions are a good start in analysing the effectiveness of current structures and channels. By reflecting on these and similar questions, you can identify current blockages and define areas for improvement.

The remaining questions on communication in this section of **QUICK WIN LEADERSHIP** give you more guidance on how to address any shortcomings identified.

See also

Q37 How can I communicate more effectively?

The phrase 'the art of communication' is widely used, but few seem to grasp just how difficult an art it is to master. Each and every day, you see people interacting and assuming that communication is happening – *"the greatest myth of communication is that it occurs"*, said George Bernard Shaw. Unfortunately, we tend to equate quantity with quality when it comes to assessing communication effectiveness. The truth is that, for all of us, our ability to communicate is a greater area for improvement than we might like to admit. Few people readily accept that they are not good communicators but, if this is the case, then:

- Why are there so many communication breakdowns in our daily lives?
- Particularly in a work context, why are there so many communication-related problems?
- Why are there so many misunderstandings and disputes?
- Why do two people often hear the same message, but end up with two differing perceptions of what it meant?

Communication is seen as a natural activity, something we learned as a small child and, perhaps, this is one of the problems; there is a mistaken belief that, because we do it all the time, in every facet of our lives, we must be good at it by now. Sadly, what happens to many of us is that, we communicate all the time but a lot of what we do is such bad practice that we steadily get worse, not better. This may seem harsh – but it is true.

To move forward in terms of communication, you first need to take a step backwards and revisit some basics. Communication is essentially about sending messages back and forth between a sender and receiver(s). Sounds simple, but clearly it is not, given all the breakdowns. The goal of any interaction must be to develop collective understanding and, unless that is achieved, real communication has not taken place. When you interact directly with another person, the messages flying back and forth are made up of three components: words, tone and body language. It is helpful to think of the messages transmitted as having two dimensions: content and context.

The *content* of your messages is provided by the words you use – the physical component of the message – whereas the *context* is delivered by your tone and body language, which define the emotional element of that message. For example, if your boss is screaming and yelling at you, are you really listening to what he / she is saying? No, more likely, you are thinking to yourself "Who does she think she is?" or "I don't get paid enough to have to put up with this". Whatever you are thinking, you are not listening to your full potential because the context of their message overshadows the content, preventing real communication from taking place. To become an effective communicator, you always must strive to ensure that the content and context of your message are in alignment.

Getting the content right
In seeking to improve how you communicate, some basic points on content include:

- Preparation is really important and the longer, or more important, the interaction you are facing, the more you need to prepare.

- Most people prepare for a formal presentation but, even for short everyday interactions, you must be clear about what you wish to say and get your thoughts organised in your own head, before you open your mouth. Think before you speak.

- It is always critical to pitch the content of what you have to say to the needs of your audience, be that one person or many. Consider what they need to know, what they know already and how best to devise the message to make it stick for them.

- Be clear, concise and do not waffle. As a general rule, people who use 10 words when two would do are poor communicators.

- Always be knowledgeable about your work and up-to-date with current trends. Take pro-active steps to build your knowledge base because this gives you the ability to frame the content of your messages better.

- When you are required to think on your feet as a communicator, split-second decisions in terms of framing content are required. However, for complex issues, where possible, do not allow yourself to be put on the spot; it is better to tell people you need to reflect on such an important matter and come back to them with an answer at a later time.

- And, when you do not have the answer on a given topic, never bluff or lie. Be honest and tell them you will get back to them when you have done some research. Then make sure you do.

- The world of work has become increasing infused with meaningless jargon, so avoid overuse of pointless phrases and buzzwords.

Aligning the context with the content

Although improving the content of your messages is relatively straightforward, managing the context of your messages is more challenging. This is because your tone and body language are emotionally-driven and, at times, even sub-conscious; as a result, it is very difficult to control, never mind manage. This is why it is usually on context that people fall down.

Managing the context of your message more effectively depends largely on your ability to remain in control of your emotions and to be assertive. People who are assertive make better communicators; it is as simple as that. When you lose control, either by becoming overly aggressive or passive, this comes out through your tone and body language as the table shows:

	Passive	Assertive	Aggressive
Tone of voice	• Quietly-spoken • Obviously nervous • Overly apologetic • Soft-spoken	• Firm • Calm • Clear	• Loud • Raised • Shouting
Words	• Talking around the subject • Avoiding getting to the issue / waffling • Overly apologetic in choice of words • Qualifying everything you say	• Concise • No waffle • Clearly expressing your opinion • Using 'I' but in a non-selfish way	• Abrupt • Threatening • Accusing • Using 'you' in a blaming fashion, • Swearing
Eyes	• Uncomfortable making eye contact • Looking down or away a lot	• Maintaining good eye contact • Not seeking to intimidate	• Staring down • Eyes bulging • Trying to intimidate
Hand gestures	• Nervous gestures • Fidgeting • Hand-wringing	• Open hand gestures	• Lots of pointing • Clenched hands • Thumping table
Body language	• Inward posture • Obviously uncomfortable • Hunched, self-protecting	• Upright posture • Head up • Using active listening	• Forward posture • In your face • Leaning • Threatening

Your inner emotions rush out through your external behaviours. This is why you need to work on your self-control as part of your attempts to become a better communicator. The critical point to note here is that positive emotions such as passion and enthusiasm are welcome, indeed essential, when trying to communicate an important message to others, so using tone and body language to reinforce what you are saying is vital at times. However, negative emotions, such as aggression, shyness or nervousness, need to be controlled because they cause you to do things with tone and body language that distract the receiver from the content of your message.

A natural starting point is to be clear on where your current areas for improvement lie; find out by soliciting feedback from others on how you communicate. Training can help, of course, but no matter how many communication seminars you attend, none of them will help you if you do not learn to control your emotions and then work hard to align your tone and all aspects of body language to reinforce your messages.

See also

Q22   What are the dangers of being too passive or aggressive as a leader?
Q35   What are the core leadership skills that contribute to success?
Q36   Why is communication so important for leaders?

Q38   What are listening skills and why are they important?

When communication is discussed, there is a tendency to focus on how we transmit messages but how we receive them is of equal importance. To become a better communicator, you also must improve your ability to listen. From a leader's perspective, consider listening:

- As a frame of mind.
- As a skill to be developed in its own right.

First, as a leader, you must be prepared always to listen to your team-members, individually and collectively. This does not mean that they can bombard you all day, every day with petty gripes, nor does it mean they can address you in terms that you consider inappropriate; just as you need to work on the context of your messages, you should never allow any of your employees to use negative emotions in how they communicate with you. But what it means is that there should be structured communication channels in place, which provide you with formal opportunities to communicate with your team on a daily, weekly and monthly basis. In addition, on a day-to-day basis, you need to make time to listen to the people around you but, again, there has to be some structure to avoid constant interruption or waste of time on trivial matters.

Second, listening is a skill that can be developed. This surprises many people because they believe that, if they have two ears and both work well, then all they need to do is to allow whatever internal process that goes on within their head to take its natural course. But, there is more to listening than that. As a skill to be developed, improving your ability to listen comprises these important elements:

- Increasing your ability to concentrate and focus, so that you minimise distractions.
- On the one hand, encouraging others who may be shy or quiet to open up, while on the other, controlling those who like to talk a lot so that they stay on the subject.

- Controlling your own natural desire to talk or respond rather than let the other person finish.

Listening is never easy because most of us have short attention spans and are easily distracted by background noise, particularly in a busy work environment. So, a first simple step you can take to help you become a better listener is to discuss important matters always in quiet, distraction-free locations.

A second difficulty in relation to listening is that the context used by others often makes it hard for us to listen. For example, some people speak in monotone voices, which can make us want to drift off; or if someone shouts at us, this also affects how we listen. Over time, you can 'educate' your team-members that you will always listen to them, but that you will never tolerate use of aggression; you will find that, slowly but surely, they will adjust their approach to you. Sadly, if the boss shouts at you, it is harder to change.

Good use of question technique with those who drone on to distraction, or stray wildly off the point, often can help to keep them, and indeed you, focused. By asking questions, you keep yourself actively involved in the interaction and you get more quickly to the heart of what they are trying to say.

Finally, becoming a better listener means using simple 'active listening' techniques, such as:

- **Maintaining eye contact:** Not only does this show you are willing to listen, but it also helps you to read body language, which often can tell you that something in the content of what the other person is saying does not stack up.
- **Nodding:** Again, this is an obvious sign that you are attentive and it encourages the speaker to keep going.
- **Encouraging:** Simply interjecting on occasion with "Yes, go on" gets them to continue to open up. This has more impact if you make eye contact; saying it while shuffling through your papers does not work!

- **Allowing short silences:** Most people hate silences and often rush to fill the gap. Do not be afraid to let short silences occur, as they let the other person know that you are not going to jump in automatically; often, this encourages them to continue talking.

- **Paraphrasing:** This means showing the person that you have got the gist of what they have said by saying things such as, "So what you are saying is ...".

- **Summarising:** This means confirming in precise detail what they have said to show that you have understood it.

Active listening is primarily about concentration and focus. Some people help us to do this because they are good communicators and make us want to listen. Others do the opposite. In a leadership role, whatever your current experience, you must strive continuously to become a better listener.

See also

Q35   What are the core leadership skills that contribute to success?
Q36   Why is communication so important for leaders?
Q37   How can I communicate more effectively?

Q39 Why are daily briefings important for leaders?

One of the easiest ways for a leader to maintain open lines of communication with their team is through the use of a daily briefing. Surprisingly, many leaders underestimate the importance of briefings and often carry them out in a haphazard way, if at all. Clearly, on its own, a 10-minute briefing held each day does not amount to much but, if held every day, then its potential is enormous; it amounts to nearly 2,500 minutes of communication with your team in a year – almost a week! So, you should consider using them more widely if you do not do so already.

A team briefing can be described as 'a system of communication that involves the leader briefly getting together with their team on a regular basis to discuss work-related matters'. Briefings can be particularly effective for:

- Communicating a common message.
- Generating respect from your team.
- Reducing misunderstandings.
- Emphasising standards on a daily basis.
- Improving teamwork.
- Encouraging openness.

Apart from allowing you to get some short, snappy messages across each day, by bringing your team together for a few minutes, you can gauge the climate and dynamic within the team – an often overlooked benefit.

Structure of a briefing

Although, they are designed to be relatively informal, you should not conduct your briefings in an *ad hoc* manner. You are 'on show' and poorly-delivered briefings make you look bad in front of your team. To make the most of your briefings, consider:

1. **Before the briefing**

   - Be clear about what you want to say; spend a few minutes thinking it through.

   - Have a set time / place for the briefing, make it a ritual – it always happens. If you cannot be present, have your second-in-command run it.

   - Always, keep it short – 10 to 15 minutes maximum.

2. **Introduction to the briefing**

   - Outline the key areas you want to discuss.

   - Encourage participation.

   - Begin on a positive note – for example, by praising work well done. Never start a briefing with a negative, as it sets a bad tone.

3. **During the briefing**

   - Be clear and concise.

   - Be enthusiastic – there is a motivational aspect to briefings, too.

   - Keep on the subject. If more substantial points come up, do not turn the briefing into a meeting but commit to putting the issue on the agenda at the next weekly meeting. Equally, if points come up that are relevant to only one or two team-members, agree to discuss those points with them directly after the briefing.

   - Check understanding by asking questions.

4. **Concluding the briefing**

   - Summarise the key points.

   - Make sure that everyone is clear about any duties / responsibilities that you have allocated.

   - Always finish on a positive note.

This simple structure will make your briefings operate more smoothly. Over time, you will see a lot of benefits from them. Furthermore, by bringing your people together each day as a unit, you reinforce the idea that you are a team and not just a collection of individuals.

See also

Q35   What are the core leadership skills that contribute to success?
Q36   Why is communication so important for leaders?
Q37   How can I communicate more effectively?
Q52   How can I motivate and engage my team-members better?

Q40   How can I manage meetings more effectively?

An unknown wit once said, "When I die, I hope it's in a meeting. The transition from life to death will be barely perceptible" – a pretty accurate description of how it feels to attend many of the meetings we all have to face at work.

You already are aware that many of the meetings you attend are ineffective, causing more frustration and eating into your limited time. As a leader, you should not inflict the same torture on your team-members.

Many leaders overlook the substantial costs, financial and non-financial, attached to failed meetings. Taking a group of employees, at any level, away from their work, even for an hour, is a significant cost in terms of productivity – and even greater when the meeting produces little of concrete value. Worse still are the hidden costs of damaged motivation and morale among those who have to attend meaningless or badly-run meetings.

And, for you personally as a leader, if your meetings are constantly ineffective, you chip away at your credibility in the eyes of your team-members – because, when a meeting fails, regardless of what actually caused that to happen, it is the leader's fault. Other people may have contributed to the poor outcome but, ultimately, the leader must take the blame. The challenge you face in terms of running an effective meeting is how to get the right balance between control and participation. Anyone can control a meeting, simply by not allowing participation, but then what would be the point?

Getting the best out of your meetings is always a challenge but there are simple steps you can take that will help. First, understand the principle of 'conditioning' in relation to meetings. All of us become conditioned to behaving and acting in particular ways when exposed to certain stimuli over a prolonged period. In meetings, this can manifest itself in many ways – for example, if your meetings always start late, then employees become conditioned that they never start on time, so they arrive late and the problem gets progressively worse. In addition, if your meetings constantly lack structure and end up going round in circles, then people become accustomed to this and come with negative expectations each time, making your role of managing the meeting even harder. If you always allow certain individuals to dominate the meeting, then you condition them into believing that they can continue to do so.

Making your meetings more effective
To make meetings more effective, consider three aspects of the meeting: before, during and after:

Before the meeting
Preparation is everything in terms of getting the foundation for the meeting right, so always consider:

- What is the purpose of the meeting / what do I want to achieve?
- Who actually needs to be there?
- What is the most appropriate time to hold the meeting?
- Where is the best place to hold the meeting?
- What will be discussed (the agenda)? What can reasonably be covered in the time available?

By ensuring that everyone knows in advance, not only what the agenda will be but also what the meeting will not be about, you start down the road to effectiveness because you set expectations appropriately.

During the meeting
Like any form of communication, your meetings must be structured – follow this basic approach:

- **Introduction:** It is important that you start your meetings on time. Do not wait for the stragglers and, when they do arrive, do not go back over what has been discussed already. If you wait for late-comers, you reward them and penalise those who do turn up on time; and, if you go back over things, you punish those who are now forced to sit through that part of the meeting a second time. But, if you condition people that your meetings start on time, very soon you will find fewer latecomers. Have a word privately with persistent latecomers and warn them that late attendance is unacceptable unless they have valid reasons – which they should inform you of before the meeting starts.

Next, you should:

- Outline the agenda points.
- Encourage participation – through you!
- Emphasise time constraints.
- Allocate responsibilities (especially a note-taker / timekeeper).

Some leaders also appoint a 'conscience' for the meeting. This is an interesting idea, as the person nominated can interrupt at any time when the meeting goes off-track to remind everyone that the point under discussion is not on the agenda. This saves you having to do it and looking like you are closing down debate. Also by appointing a note-taker, timekeeper and conscience, you change the dynamic from one person controlling the meeting (you) to four people contributing to making the meeting more effective. Obviously, if you use this approach, rotate the positions for each meeting.

- **Main part:** Here, you need to work hard to get the right balance between control and participation. In the beginning, it is important that you prevent any unacceptable behaviours from going unopposed; to do otherwise, creates an impression that they are acceptable. You may have to be quite 'steering' in the beginning but stick with it as you will find these negative type behaviours will disappear from your meetings over time.

In working through the content of the meeting, always introduce each agenda point and frame the discussion. By doing this, you focus the conversation and also can point out what will and will not be discussed under that agenda point.

As the discussion develops, it is up to you to:

- Maintain control / participation.
- Keep the discussion on track.
- Allow involvement from all participants, who should wait to be brought into the discussion, so only one person talks at a time.
- Prevent disagreements from getting out of hand, without stifling healthy debate.

- Keep to the allocated time.

To ensure clarity as to the outcome of agenda points, you must summarise any agreement / action for each point before moving to the next. Agreed actions should then be noted by the note-taker.

- **Conclusion:** Managing a meeting effectively means that it finishes on time; or, at the very least, that when the allocated time is reached, a conscious decision is made to extend it. At the end of a meeting, you should summarise all the points agreed, ensuring that each participant is clear on the action they must take following the meeting and the completion date for same. Thank everyone for attending and for participating.

After the meeting
After the meeting, ensure that the action plan is circulated and that any action agreed is implemented within the agreed timeframe. Failure to do so sends out the message that nothing happens as a result of your meetings, which lowers expectations for future meetings.

Finally, feedback is always good, so do not be afraid to ask your team-members on an ongoing basis for their comments on how they feel the meeting went and any proposals they might have for subsequent meetings.

Following these simple steps will ensure that, over time, the quality and effectiveness of your meetings will improve.

See also

Q35   What are the core leadership skills that contribute to success?
Q36   Why is communication so important for leaders?
Q37   How can I communicate more effectively?

Q41 Why are presentation skills so critical in a leadership role?

The ability to deliver a compelling presentation is an important skill that all leaders require, to some extent at least. You must build your capabilities, confidence and technique to present in front of a group of people, formally and informally, because inability to do so affects your credibility. Every time you make a presentation, you practice your general communication skills and develop your assertiveness and self-confidence, so you should seek to present to others as often as you can.

For many people, even experienced professionals, public speaking to any group, be it small or large, can be quite stressful; it is a common fear. But, with a bit of structure, some basic techniques and lots of practice, there is no reason why anything should go wrong. Many of the causes of failed presentations are easily avoided – often, they are due to shortcomings in two areas: lack of preparation and poor delivery.

Preparation
When preparing for a presentation, ask yourself:

- What message do I want to convey? (**Content**)
- Why am I conveying this message? (**Purpose**)
- Who will I be making the presentation to? What do they know already about the subject? (**Audience**)
- How am I going to get my point across?(**Delivery**)
- When will the presentation take place and how long do I have? (**Timing**)
- Where will I be making the presentation? (**Location**)

These questions will help you to clarify your thoughts. Always begin your preparation by defining a clear objective for the talk; how you then structure, and indeed deliver, that talk should be geared totally towards achieving your objective.

The following structure can help to map out the content of your talk:

- **Introduction:** The initial impression you create during your talk is very important, so you should keep that in mind as you prepare. You will gain or lose the attention of your audience by what you say in the first few minutes. In your introduction, plan to tell them:
  - What you are going to talk about.
  - The key points you will cover.
  - How long your talk will last.
  - How you propose to deal with their questions (during or after?).
  - Highlight whether you have supporting documentation to give them or whether they need to take notes.

  Some presenters like to include an attention-grabbing statement, or use humour early in their presentation to attract the audience. This can be a good idea, depending upon the nature of the presentation of course, and only if you can pull it off. If you are not comfortable with humour, do not think you suddenly can turn into a comedian.

- **Development:** As you sit down to prepare the main part of your presentation, think first about all the information you *could* give the audience on the topic (you might use a 'buzz map', or brainstorming to help you with this). Then consider your objective, what they might know already and narrow down your points by thinking about what you *must* and *should* tell them in order to achieve that objective. Also keep in mind the time available to you, as this naturally impacts on what you can include. As you lay out the points, the main body should always follow a logical sequence, so give some thought to how you will structure your points in clear stages to give an overall 'flow' to the talk. Also, consider the use of visual aids such as PowerPoint, whiteboards or flipcharts; whatever you use, it is important not to have too many visual aids and to ensure that they are of good quality, easy to understand, and easy to read. In a long talk, add in some re-caps as part of the main body.

- **Conclusion:** Your presentation should always include a summary at the end, as it is important to refresh all the key points for your audience. Once you have summarised your key points, when delivering your presentation, you should thank your audience and allow them to ask you questions.

Allocate time to each of the three sections roughly along these lines: Introduction (10%), Development (80%), Conclusion (10%). If questions are included in the overall time, then adjust these timings somewhat.

Delivery

Having a structure, quality but brief notes and appropriate visual aids prepared will give you confidence that you know what you want to say. Then, it is a matter of practice, practice, practice; run through the presentation in front of colleagues, family or friends and even in front of the mirror at home. This will help you to be more relaxed on the day and you also will find out whether you have got the timing right.

For more formal presentations, keep these tips in mind:
Before you present

- Remember the importance of your appearance when communicating. Make sure you look your best and choose clothes that are appropriate for the expected formality of the occasion.

- If you are unfamiliar with the venue for the presentation, visit it in advance (if you can). Also check out the audio-visual facilities, making sure they can accommodate your needs.

- Ensure that any notes you have prepared are easy to read, perhaps even written on small cards; but do not have too many notes either, as they will detract from your interaction with the audience.

- Arrive early on the day, set up in plenty of time to do a dry-run.

- Once you have set up and completed your dry-run, spend some time on your own. Get some fresh air and try to think of something else. Try to replace any negative thoughts with positive ones.

- About 15 minutes before you are due to start, do a quick double check that everything is ready – remember Murphy's law. Take all coins, keys, pens, etc. out of your pockets at this point – to prevent you jangling them during the presentation. Give a final check to your appearance – make sure you look the part.

- Take some deep breaths, and sip some cold water. Also make sure that you have some water close to you during the presentation, in case your mouth dries up; if that happens, stop and take a sip.

During the presentation

- Continuously make good eye contact with all your audience; do not just focus on one area.

- Speak clearly, and at an even pace, but do not shout. Vary the tone of your voice and emphasise key words. If you use a microphone, match the pitch of your voice to the power of the sound system.

- Movement can be good during the presentation, but avoid moving too quickly, rocking side-to-side or other nervous movements.

- Use positive hand gestures to support your message, but make sure they support what you say, and do not distract from it.

- When using your visual aids, look at the audience and do not turn your back to face the screen.

- Keep your hands away from your mouth when you are talking.

- Do not fiddle with your pen, notes, pointers, etc; this will distract people and highlight your nervousness.

- Again, if you use humour during the talk, make sure it is appropriate and, more importantly, make sure it is funny.

- Remember, even if you think you appear very nervous, it is rarely as bad as you imagine. If you have prepared well, you will do well.

These simple points will help you to prepare and deliver a winning presentation. As soon as you can after the presentation, review your own performance. Think about how you could improve for the next one. Also, if you know some of the audience well, ask them for their opinion. Constructive feedback helps to enhance future performance.

See also

Q35   What are the core leadership skills that contribute to success?
Q36   Why is communication so important for leaders?
Q37   How can I communicate more effectively?

Q42   How can I write reports professionally?

Any leader needs the ability to write clear, concise and effective reports; depending upon your role, these can vary from one-page summaries of events to comprehensive strategic documents. A report can be defined as *"a document in which a given problem or situation is examined for the purpose of conveying information, reporting findings, putting forward ideas and sometimes making recommendations"*.

In writing any report, three golden rules apply:

- Accuracy.
- Brevity.
- Clarity.

In particular, as you are committing something to paper, you need to be factually accurate so that you can stand by it if challenged.

The basic 3Ps approach to writing a report will help you to prepare and present a useful document.

Preparation

- Be very clear on what you have been asked to do. If there are terms of reference, study them carefully and get clarification if necessary.
- Identify what is already known on the subject and where the gaps lie – where you can add value.
- Develop your research plan on that basis.
- Complete all your research before you even contemplate writing the document – have the full picture first.

Planning

Think long and hard about how you will structure and present the information. This sounds very obvious, but many people start to write and then structure as they go along; this often leads to a disjointed report. When planning how to structure the document, consider:

- Who are the primary, and possibly secondary, audiences for the report?
- What do they already know about the subject? There is no point structuring the report in a way that much of it simply tells the reader what they know already.
- How best to get your points across?

In planning the report, make sure that you structure it in line with the terms of reference. For example, if the report requests proposals, then there should be a strong link from the findings of the research to each and every one of your proposals. Many people provide information, or worse still, baseless personal opinions in reports when they were not requested.

Presentation
The presentation of reports depend on their purpose, scope and length but usually follow this general flow:

- Title.
- Summary (particularly if a long report).
- Introduction (terms of reference and methodology explained).
- Main body (structured depending upon what is required).
- Conclusions.
- Recommendations (if requested).

Before presenting the report, you must ensure that it contains no spelling or grammatical errors or other inaccuracies and that any tables and charts included are of high quality. This may seem like a point that does not require a mention but, unfortunately, the reality is that many work-related reports and internal documents do not reflect well on the person who prepared them.

See also
Q35   What are the core leadership skills that contribute to success?
Q36   Why is communication so important for leaders?
Q37   How can I communicate more effectively?

Q43 How can I improve my negotiation skills?

Work-life revolves around various forms of negotiation, so the ability to lead formal and informal negotiations comprises a significant part of any leadership role. Although negotiations can take many formats, and have many purposes, the real art of negotiation is to arrive at an outcome that both parties are happy with or, at the very least, can live with.

A model for handling more formal negotiations is provided here. However, these general guidelines can be pared back to apply in less formal situations – for example, if you were negotiating with a team-member regarding a pay rise.

Preparing to negotiate
Key tasks to be considered include:

- Clarify your objectives for the negotiations. What are you hoping to get from the negotiation? What is your bottom line?

- Decide which issues are open to compromise and which are not; thus defining your areas of flexibility. If you have no areas of flexibility, the negotiations become more difficult because you are not actually willing to negotiate.

- Research as much relevant information on the subject under negotiation as possible – the more you know about the issue, the more confident you will feel. Are there previous agreements in place with the opposite party that might be relevant?

- Talk to others who may have negotiated with the other party previously, to gain insights into their likely approach; the more you know about the opposition, the better.

- Think also about the likely case to be presented by the other party, its potential strengths and weaknesses.

- Define your own strategy and, if others are supporting you, ensure that all the negotiating team are clear on their roles during the negotiations.

Other factors to be considered in preparation are the location for the negotiations and its implications, as well as the timings and general logistics to be arranged. An agenda for the negotiations ideally should be agreed between both parties in advance.

Conducting the negotiations

Ensure from the outset that the right atmosphere is created. Negotiations do not have to be held in an 'icy' atmosphere, although this is often a tactic used. The early stages of the negotiations should be designed to ensure that all parties are familiar with each other and some sort of rapport is developed between them. If not already agreed, it is critical to agree the format for the negotiations and any relevant logistics at this stage.

The remainder of the negotiations cannot be outlined easily, as the format depends upon the nature of the negotiation, the complexity of the issues, the degree of distance between each party, the numbers involved and even the approaches taken by the individuals attending. However, there are some common stages:

- **Opening positions:** The parties begin by stating their opening positions, usually with some in-built flexibility for them (their best case scenario).

- **Negotiation:** This phase involves discussion, bargaining, debate, offer and counter-offer before agreement can be reached. The bulk of the debate focuses on the problem areas, but it can be advisable to identify any common ground early. If things get difficult later and an impasse is reached, it can be useful to return to these areas of mutual agreement. During the negotiation process, it is important too to focus on the opposition's position rather than their personalities. Be aware that many tactics are adopted by each side in pursuit of their objectives. Also, it is important that you summarise each parties' position on a regular basis, to ensure there is no backtracking at a later stage. These summaries also help to identify whether the parties are moving closer or further apart.

- **Confirmation:** It is essential to get full agreement from both parties on the results of the negotiations. This reduces the likelihood of either party reneging on the deal at a later stage or subsequently adopting a different position. The next steps in the process should be clearly defined to ensure any agreements are implemented.

These steps are a simplified framework for negotiations but are a useful guide nonetheless. There can be many twists and turns in achieving final agreement, with emotions, personalities and behaviours all playing a vital part. It is important to recognise this psychological element involved in the negotiating process. Ultimately, it is only through practical experience that you can really enhance your negotiation skills.

See also

Q35   What are the core leadership skills that contribute to success?
Q36   Why is communication so important for leaders?
Q37   How can I communicate more effectively?

Q44   Why are influencing and persuading skills important?

Influencing and persuading others is about changing their views, attitudes or actions without having to rely on your position or authority, or coercion. It is a critical skill for leaders in dealing with their team, but perhaps more so in their interactions with colleagues, superiors and customers.

Your ability to influence and persuade others is not really a separate set of skills – there are techniques, for sure – but your ability to bring others round to your point of view is determined by a range of factors. For example, you can never hope to influence others unless some basic building blocks are in place:

- **Credibility:** You have to have credibility in the eyes of others, if you hope to exert influence over them.

- **Trust / integrity:** If people do not trust you, or if you lack integrity, then you can forget about influencing others in a positive way.

- **Passion and enthusiasm:** Without these qualities, your ability to influence others is limited.

- **Empathy:** Unless you can put yourself in the shoes of others, you will find it hard to develop arguments that respond to their needs.

- **Personal skills and attributes:** Your ability to influence and persuade others is not something that you turn on and off as required; instead, many of the leadership attributes highlighted elsewhere in **QUICK WIN LEADERSHIP** are relevant here too.

Persuading others specifically relates to your ability to define and deliver compelling arguments that serve to bring others towards your way of thinking, whilst at the same time satisfying some particular need or expectation they may have. Again, how good you are at doing this depends on your overall effectiveness as a communicator, your level of knowledge and insight into a particular subject and your ability to be assertive.

A basic assumption when seeking to influence and persuade others is that you can devise a strong case that creates a win-win situation for both parties and then that you can make that case to others in a manner appealing to them. Some important considerations when seeking to influence or persuade include:

- Define clearly what you really want to achieve.
- Be clear on who has the power to deliver what you want and indeed who can put obstacles in your way.
- Understand the frames of mind of others and identify what needs your proposals can satisfy for them.
- Build a strong case that bridges the gap between your objective and the current position, while delivering tangible benefits for others.
- Define those key benefits for others in terms that will be meaningful for them – be specific, not vague.
- Deliver your case with passion and enthusiasm.
- Be prepared for objections, listen to them when raised and address those concerns by offering tangible solutions.
- Do not attempt to oversell your proposals.

In a work context, as well as influencing employees, colleagues and customers, you will need to be able to influence and persuade your superiors, particularly on occasions when you are seeking extra resources, or attempting to get support for change. Clearly, this poses additional challenges for you because the authority completely lies with them; as such, you are totally reliant on your talents for persuasion. Be conscious in these circumstances that your chances of success are increased when you make a strong business, not an emotional, case for what you are seeking. In addition, when communicating up the chain, the nature of, and indeed the language used within, your argument is vital. Below are some examples of good and bad choices of words when seeking to influence up the chain of command.

Terms to Avoid	Terms to use
• "We need this". • "Everybody else is spending €X, so we will be left behind". • "It will make a major difference to the business". • "We could lose a lot of good people if we don't do this". • "It will improve the quality of our service". • "Morale will be better if we do this". • "Our customers will be more loyal if we do this".	• "This additional resource will cost us €X but will lead to an increase of sales of €Y in six months". • "Since our competitors implemented this approach, they have grown their market share by 5% over us". • "By investing in this project, it will deliver the following benefits immediately ...". • "Employee turnover is currently X. By changing this system, we can reduce that to Y in six months, which will yield savings of Z". • "Research undertaken among our customers has indicated that 75% of them would increase their purchases if we offered this product".

Given the changing dynamics of work today, as a leader you are called upon to influence and persuade far more often than someone in your position 20 years ago. With growing pressures on resources, financial and otherwise, within organisations, you have to make a much stronger case for what you want than might have been the case previously, so work hard to develop your ability to influence and persuade.

See also

Q23   Why do leaders need to be passionate and enthusiastic?
Q27   Why is empathy important to a leader?
Q28   Why is integrity essential for leaders?
Q35   What are the core leadership skills that contribute to success?
Q36   Why is communication so important for leaders?
Q37   How can I communicate more effectively?

Q45　How can I develop my problem-solving skills?

Problem-solving is a significant part of any leader's role and can involve dealing with both minor and major issues on an ongoing basis. Some problems require little thought, as the solution is fairly obvious – but make sure, even when faced with minor difficulties, that you choose the best, and not just the most obvious, or convenient, solution. At the other end of the scale, leaders are regularly confronted by major problems – for these, you need to be very structured in your thinking.

Here are some key steps to keep in mind:

- **Identify the real problem:** It sounds obvious that, to solve a problem, you need first to define what it is, but it is easy to fall into the trap of focusing more on symptoms, rather than the root cause.

- **Establish all the facts:** Having defined the problem, then explore it in detail and learn as much about it as you can. You must consult, investigate, research and analyse it from all angles until you have the full picture – or as much of it as possible, given the time available to you for research.

- **Consider all the options:** When the facts are known, then shift your focus to defining an appropriate solution. Avoid 'straight-line' thinking and a rush to the most obvious solution. This stage provides an ideal opportunity for creativity.

- **Establish the likely impact of each option:** For each potential solution identified, evaluate the advantages and disadvantages, including both their likely immediate and longer-term impact.

- **Select and implement the best option:** Having evaluated all the alternatives, select and plan the implementation of the agreed solution. And, afterwards, monitor progress and ensure that any blockages to implementation are dealt with effectively.

See also

Q35　What are the core leadership skills that contribute to success?

Q46 How and when should I delegate?

Delegation is not the same as getting others to do your work, although it is often confused with it. Certain duties fall naturally to subordinates, and the only action needed by the leader is to decide which member of the team should be given the work, depending on workload, etc – this allocation of duties is a normal part of the leader's role. At the other end of the scale lies abdication, which means the leader dumps meaningless work on others that he / she could not be bothered doing – do not do this.

Delegation is entirely different. It involves devolving responsibility to others for tasks that are substantial in nature and are not normally part of their duties, but will help them to develop in some way. By delegating that task, the leader frees up time that allows them to focus on other more important tasks. Delegation is a win-win situation: the employee learns new things and builds their capabilities; for the leader, delegation plays an important role in their overall ability to manage their time – and so, you should maximise its use.

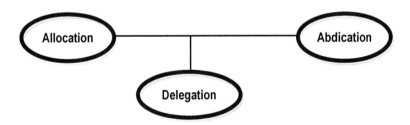

When you delegate a task, you devolve the responsibility for its completion but remain accountable for that task; after all, it is part of your duties not the employee's. Therefore, consider the following points:

- **Select the right person:** Not all employees want to be delegated to, so you need to define the right person and ask them whether they would like to take the task on. You cannot force them to do it, as it falls under your remit.

- **Delegation is a process:** When you first delegate the task, you are likely to lose time, not gain it. You will have to spend time with the individual to train and coach them, communicating how to do it and the outcomes required and supporting them initially as they get to grips with it.

- **Delegate authority relevant to the job:** If the task requires your employee to request support and assistance from others, it is important that you communicate to all concerned that you have delegated responsibility to them for this task; otherwise, the employee may be faced with difficulties when requesting that support.

Analyse your job

↓

Decide what to delegate

↓

Select the right person

↓

Communicate the delegation

↓

Review the delegation

- **Monitor and review but do not micro-manage:** Since you remain accountable for the task, you must follow up to ensure it is completed but, once you are confident that your team-member is competent at it, do not stand over their shoulder constantly. Obviously, it goes without saying that you should offer praise for a job well done.

Delegation, when managed correctly, is a powerful tool for both you and some of your employees. By following these commonsense guidelines, you can avoid the common pitfalls associated with delegating and maximise the potential of individuals within your team eager to develop their talents. As a leader, you will see a major return for the effort you put into delegating effectively.

See also

Q35   What are the core leadership skills that contribute to success?

Q47 How can I become a better planner?

Part of every leader's role involves planning, and the significance of that planning naturally increases as you rise through the ranks. At more junior levels, you may be responsible for planning workload over the short-term; at mid-level, you may be involved in annual planning; whereas at senior level, your role as a leader will include strategic planning. Add to this the need to plan your own time in order to be effective and you can see that planning is, and will continue to be, an important skill for you. Without effective planning, you will have no clear direction – be that personal or organisationally; nor will you have any means of measuring success. When you fail to plan, as the old saying goes, you plan to fail.

Factors affecting planning decisions
Whatever level of planning you are currently involved in, you should consider the following questions to help you improve your ability to plan:

- Do you have good awareness of the business environment relevant to your position in the organisation?
- Is there accurate, up-to-date management information available to you to help guide your planning decisions?
- Do you understand that information and are you comfortable interpreting it?
- Are there specific objectives and targets defined to guide your planning decisions?
- Do you have access to appropriate planning tools?

In seeking to improve your planning skills, you should consider planning, at any level, to be about finding answers to four basic questions:

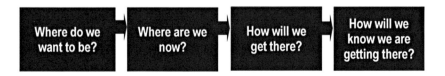

Where do we want to be? → Where are we now? → How will we get there? → How will we know we are getting there?

Planning is about trying to move yourself, or your organisation, towards outcomes. To do so means you have to determine what those desired outcomes might be; at junior level, these may be provided for you but, at senior level, you are responsible for defining measurable goals and targets. Based on where you want to be, you then examine the current position – what are the gaps in relation to the expected outcomes? From that, you plan the necessary actions to help bridge those gaps, reviewing and monitoring progress at regular intervals.

Personal planning

Planning skills include the ability to plan your own time. Here are some simple steps to increase your efficiency through better time management:

- **Improve your time planning:** Every leader needs some tools to help them plan their time and whether that is a diary, Blackberry or Outlook, the tool is less important than the rationale behind it. It is more important for you to define your priority actions to be addressed on any given day. At the end of each day, you review your list and follow the same approach day after day. By doing so, you ultimately build up your efficiency levels.

- **Reduce your time wastage:** If you look objectively at any work day, there is always some wastage of time, perhaps not through your fault, but nonetheless eating into your available time. Whether this waste arises from having to sit through a fruitless meeting, wading through endless emails or constant interruptions, by reflecting on how you could reduce wastages within your control, you can find some areas for improvement.

- **Delegation:** By delegating in an effective manner, you can free up your time to tackle those priority issues directly related to achieving your defined goals.

See also

Q35   What are the core leadership skills that contribute to success?
Q46   How and when should I delegate?

Q48 How might I use mentoring and networking as tools to help me grow as a leader?

The leadership role is a challenging one that requires you to update your skills and knowledge constantly throughout your career. At times, it can be lonely, if you do not have supports within your organisation to help you cope with the not insignificant hurdles you face or, even when they are available, you may not always feel comfortable discussing issues internally, in case you are seen in a negative light. And so, it is useful for leaders to develop their networks to the full and to seek mentors to guide them.

Networking

Effective networking can contribute significantly to your personal development and in helping you to gain access to new opportunities and positions. Three types of networks may be valuable to you:

- **Internal networks:** There always are key people within any organisation with whom you should strive to develop meaningful relationships, not only in a political sense, but in terms of forging bonds with those who play an integral part in helping you to deliver on your leadership responsibilities and achieve your goals.

- **External business networks:** There are many business associations and online networks, each targeting a specific field. You should be a member of the most important bodies relevant to your industry. You should also search for networks where other leaders are prevalent, as these can be useful contacts for you in sharing and learning from common experiences.

- **Social networks:** Do not neglect this aspect of your life.

Some people misunderstand – and misuse – networking, so it is important that you use it for the right reason and in the right way. There is nothing worse than someone who tries to network solely out of self-interest. Keep these simple points in mind:

- View networking as a two-way process – do not simply search for new contacts for what you might get out of the relationship.

- Take a long-term view – networking rarely delivers immediate results.
- Always be prepared to help your contacts, without seeking an immediate pay-back.
- Networking is not the same as handing out your business card to all and sundry.
- You must be pro-active in sustaining your network.

Mentoring

Mentoring is another potential support mechanism for leaders; some organisations have formal programmes in place, whereby senior leaders mentor those more junior to them. In the absence of a formal structure, you can identify your own mentors either inside or outside the company.

To get the full value of mentoring, ensure that you:

- Carefully choose your mentor(s); always identify individuals whom you know and respect as leaders, or for their specific expertise.
- Determine the precise areas that each mentor can help you with. One mentor cannot meet all your support needs.
- Stay clearly focused upon specific development needs.

Most people you approach will be happy to serve as a mentor and then it is a matter of determining what time they can devote to the role.

Although mentoring relationships should be relatively informal, they should not be *ad hoc*. Therefore, in managing the relationship, clarify both parties' expectations, the specific focus of the mentoring, how often you will meet and how you might measure progress. By simple preparation and planning steps such as these, you will enhance the results you get.

See also

Q35   What are the core leadership skills that contribute to success?
Q89   How can I establish a leadership mentoring programme within the organisation?

LEADING INDIVIDUALS AND TEAMS

Q49   What makes an effective team?

Many elements combine to create an effective team. One key determinant is the quality of leadership, so how effectively you lead your people has a direct impact on how well they bind as a team. Accordingly, working constantly to improve your skills as a leader should be your personal contribution to the teambuilding process.

As shown in the diagram above, priority concerns in this regard include:

- **Common goals:** A team without common goals is a team in name only. Your role as leader is to work with your team-members to define meaningful and relevant common goals.

- **Collaboration:** An effective team is noted for the high levels of co-operation and collaboration seen between team-members. As leader, you can play an active role in building these levels.

- **Compatibility:** Of course, not all team-members will like each other to the same degree, but there must be some element of compatibility between them. This has implications for you in terms of how you recruit new team-members to ensure they 'fit' as closely as possible with existing employees.

- **Commitment:** Unless all team-members are committed to the team, and its goals, disharmony may result. Levels of commitment may fluctuate to some extent, but you should never tolerate any individual who shows continuous lack of commitment to the team, either in terms of their attitude, behaviour or overall productivity.

- **Communication:** The best teams always have high levels of meaningful and productive communication between them. As leader, you should ensure the right structures and channels are in place to maximise the effectiveness of internal communication.

- **Climate:** A broad area that has to do with general levels of morale, how problems are dealt with, trust and other issues that set the general tone for the working environment. In many ways, a positive climate is the output from the other factors but, in your role as leader, you can contribute to creating the right climate through your own attitude and behaviour. You should monitor the climate constantly and, when you identify blockages, act proactively to address them.

This is not an exhaustive list of factors that contribute to an effective team but they are key areas that you always should pay significant attention to.

See also

Q36   Why is communication so important for leaders?
Q50   How do teams change and develop over time?
Q51   What is the difference between organisation culture and climate?

Q50   How do teams change and develop over time?

Teams are not static entities; they evolve and change over time, depending on the prevailing environment. Tuckman's stages of team development – forming, storming, norming and performing – is one model that describes how teams develop, or not, as the case may be. However, while this is a useful framework for a project team, where all members come together at the one time and stay in place for the duration, it is not wholly appropriate in the workplace where teams are constantly changing as individuals join and leave.

As an alternative, rather than view team development from this progressive model perspective, consider differing states of team effectiveness. After all, a team is judged on its ability to achieve the required outcomes, not necessarily on how long it has been in existence.

Using the same parameters as for the leadership styles model in **Q32**, three states of team effectiveness, and their implications for leadership style, can be considered:

States of Team Effectiveness

- **Ineffective state:** At times, teams can be described as being *ineffective* in terms of achieving outcomes or in bonding together, perhaps due to the fact that many of the members are new, or because there has been a breakdown within the team of some kind. Equally, a new work practice might have been introduced and the team could be considered ineffective on that activity until they have mastered the new approach. In reality, many factors can make a team ineffective and no team can excel on all occasions.

- **Excelling state:** At the opposite end of the scale, a team might be deemed *excelling* when it is working well as a unit and outcomes are being achieved that surpass expectations. All teams can go through a 'purple patch' at times, where everything just runs to perfection. Of course, the ideal is to build up a team that excels most of the time.

- **Effective state:** In the middle, a team can be described as *effective*, which means it is working well and delivering on expectations.

These three states perhaps are a more accurate portrayal of what happens in the real world when it comes to teams in the workplace. Rather than progress through definable stages, teams can shift back and forth through the three states.

Viewing teams as fluctuating between different states of effectiveness is also useful from a leader's perspective, as it can give you some guidance regarding what leadership style to apply. Where a team is ineffective, you need to adopt the *steering* style of leadership until you have them performing at the level you want. An effective team responds best to an *engaging* style of leadership, while a team that is excelling will be ready for the *facilitating* leadership style.

Reflect on your own team, or if not already a leader, think of the team you currently work in:

- What state(s) of effectiveness does it operate in most of the time? Are there wild fluctuations? What causes these fluctuations?

- How does your (or your leader's) leadership style vary in response?

- What might be done differently to keep the team in an effective state more of the time, or to progress it to an excelling state?

- How does the climate in the team change with the state of effectiveness?

As a leader, it is important that you monitor your team's state of effectiveness constantly and take pro-active measures to address any blockages that you find.

See also

Q49   What makes an effective team?

Q51   What is the difference between organisation culture and climate?

It can be difficult to distinguish between organisation culture and climate without getting drawn into theoretical or abstract analysis. They are intangible features of organisation life and, although hard to put into simple terms, they are vital concepts for leaders to understand.

Culture is the foundation upon which any organisation is built. It develops over the longer term and consists of the values (stated and implicit), beliefs, norms and traditions that guide how the organisation does its business and, in turn, how people behave. In simple terms, it is the 'personality' of the organisation and, often, the culture of an organisation can be traced back to the personal values held by the founder or the senior management. Although it is intangible, culture has a significant role in influencing all aspects of life within the organisation and, indeed, how it interacts with the outside world; think how the culture of a Wall Street brokerage firm differs from that of a charitable organisation.

Climate, on the other hand, is something more surface level, relating to the here-and-now; it is about what it feels like to work in the organisation. If culture is the personality, then climate is the mood or prevailing atmosphere within the business. The climate is prone to more short-term fluctuations and is determined by many factors, including leadership, structure, rewards and recognition.

Understanding the difference between culture and climate is helpful for you as a leader. Changing culture is a significant challenge, and may be out of your hands, depending upon your seniority. However, you can influence the climate within your team by how you lead them; your overall leadership style, how you design or improve work practices, recognise and reward performance and how conflict is handled all impact on climate.

See also

Q32   What are the different leadership styles?

Q49   What makes an effective team?
Q58   How can I deal more effectively with conflict?
Q61   How should I recognise and reward my employees?

Q52   How can I motivate and engage my team-members better?

One of the most common questions asked by leaders is "How can I motivate my people?".

The key components to motivating others are:

- Leading your people to the best of your ability.
- Addressing obvious factors such as your leadership style, how you communicate and involve your team, what climate is created in the organisation, the basic working conditions and so on.
- Get to know your team members so that you can pinpoint their individual motivators.

By addressing these issues, you raise satisfaction levels with work and, from there, it is easier to motivate people.

When attempting to motivate your people, consider the following questions:

- Do you lead your people in a way that enhances their potential to be motivated and engaged?
- Are you getting all the basics right that contribute to employee motivation?
- Do you really know each of your team-members and what might be some of their individual motivators?
- How are any financial rewards that operate in your team structured? Do they serve as a motivation for the majority and not just for a few?

Not everyone can be motivated to the same degree; some do not need to be motivated because they can self-motivate, others can be relatively easily motivated, whereas a few prove very difficult to motivate at all. As a leader, remember that the bottom line for all employees is that they consistently do what is expected of them to the standard required. That is what they are paid to do; that is what they must do.

When you ask employees what motivates them, money is usually high up on the list. But delve a bit deeper, and you find that money, or the fixed-pay element at least, is a satisfier not a motivator. When someone thinks they are underpaid for what they do, they tend to be dissatisfied with their job, and not motivated to the fullest extent. But if they suddenly received a big pay rise, would they be more motivated? More satisfied for certain, but more motivated? Maybe in the short run, yes, but sooner or later, they would want more money again. So, at best, money is a short-term motivator. Performance-related pay can be a longer-term motivator but poorly-structured schemes based only on individual reward can lead to a focus on the individual and not the team and thus to decreased motivation overall.

In terms of motivating all individuals, as well as higher level factors such as overall work conditions, culture and the nature of leader-employee relationships, there are simple points to consider too that are always directly within your control. Positive feedback and a simple 'Thank you', when deserved, go a long way. So too does taking a personal interest in your people and showing that you are willing to listen to them or support them when needed. Don't overlook the motivational power of getting the basics right.

See also

Q32   What are the different leadership styles?
Q49   What makes an effective team?
Q61   How should I recognise and reward my employees?
Q86   What is employee engagement?
Q87   How can I increase employee engagement levels?
Q88   How might I measure employee engagement?

Q53 How can I foster greater collaboration amongst my team-members?

On a practical level, there are a number of things you can do to enhance collaboration and your ability to make the most of them depends upon how closely in tune you are with the overall team dynamic:

- **Work allocation:** On a daily basis, when you allocate various tasks and projects, be conscious of how you distribute the workload. If, for example, you find that certain individuals tend to relate more closely together at the expense of others, then try to get these team-members working with different people. This 'mix-and-match' approach can break down barriers and help your team to get to know one and other better.

- **Role discovery:** Often misunderstandings develop between team-members simply because they do not understand precisely what each other does, or the pressures and strains associated with other roles. Although it does taking planning and has costs attached, for example, allowing a sales employee to spend a half-day shadowing someone in the accounts section and *vice versa* can help people to understand their respective roles and responsibilities better and break down significant inter-team barriers.

- **Team-based problem-solving:** When a significant problem is identified, why not bring a few team-members together – particularly those who may not usually work side-by-side – provide them with direction and ask them to come up with suggestions as to how the problem might be resolved.

Consistently applying these approaches will foster greater levels of collaboration.

In addition, as the leader of the team, you should request resources from your superiors to conduct occasional formal team-building events that can be designed and delivered in response to specific team-related problems you may be facing.

Overall, take every opportunity to reinforce the notion that you are a team. You can do this subtly through holding daily briefings, weekly meetings and even through the odd social outing.

See also

Q49   What makes an effective team?

Q54 How should I deal with difficult individuals in the team?

The term 'difficult' can cover a multitude of sins but, regardless of how an employee is underperforming, the general steps in addressing the issue are broadly the same.

First, if you do not deal with the problem, your inactivity will have a detrimental effect on the team as a whole. For example, allowing an employee to get away with producing shoddy work makes others question why they should bother making the effort to do it right.

Always start with an open mind and abide by the principles of fairness and natural justice; everyone should be given a chance, and support if required, to improve. But, if they fail to respond to that opportunity, there must be clear consequences.

A general framework for resolving these matters is:

- **Recognition:** First draw the employee's attention to the problem and make it clear that you will no longer tolerate it. Draw a line in the sand, so to speak.

- **Acceptance:** An important early step is to get the employee to accept that there is a problem. Often this can be difficult, as some individuals are unaware of what they are doing, or will attempt to deny it or blame it on someone else. But, if they refuse to be accountable, then you must make it clear that there is a problem and that they need to resolve it.

- **Discussion:** Some degree of discussion is always necessary because simply telling someone to get their act together does not usually work. You are prepared to be supportive here, to listen, to evaluate but you should not allow yourself to be taken for a fool either.

- **Action:** Based on the discussion, either agree what they need to change, or impose the route forward. Some action may required on your behalf too, as valid issues may have arisen that contribute to the problem and therefore require attention from you.

- **Review:** Always ensure that you review their performance at defined intervals to ensure that they are addressing the problem. If they fail to live up to their commitments, or fail to abide by what you were forced to impose, then do not rehash the whole problem again. You have given them a chance, the necessary support and they have not responded. You now must move to applying whatever disciplinary process is relevant in your organisation.

Essentially, start with a coaching-type approach but, if that does not work, shift to a disciplinary-based solution.

It is important to begin with coaching, not only out of natural fairness, but also due to the fact that once you go the disciplinary route, the nature of the relationship changes and there is likely to be no way back because, if nothing else, you have made up your mind that they no longer fit in the team.

See also

Q56   How should I discipline team-members?
Q63   How should I coach my employees to improved performance?

Q55   How should I handle employee grievances?

Grievances take many forms but generally relate to a feeling of dissatisfaction or injustice concerning some aspect of the work relationship. The majority of grievances are minor in nature and usually are taken care of as a matter of course by the leader during their normal working day. However, from time to time, you can be faced with something more serious and potentially more damaging to the employee, to you as the leader or to the organisation as a whole. In these situations, you need to be seen to treat it seriously and also to ensure that all parties' interests are protected.

Serious grievances usually arise from an employee feeling isolated, abused, harassed or discriminated against in some way for a prolonged period. Rarely, if you are leading your team well, will a serious problem arise out of the blue. Given the potential severity of some of these grievances, companies usually have a formal procedure in place; naturally, you must adhere to whatever framework is in place within your organisation.

In doing so, keep in mind these points:

- Even for minor grievances, treat the complaint seriously. Often minor issues grow into bigger concerns because the employee felt that their leader did not give the matter the attention it deserved.
- For more serious grievances, put the details in writing and have the employee sign the record.
- Keep the employee informed at all stages as to what action is being taken, so that they know the matter is being dealt with.
- Always involve your superiors and / or your human resources department in serious matters.
- Investigate the issue fully, where appropriate using an independent third party.
- Never victimise the employee for bringing up the grievance, regardless of the outcome.

- If the grievance is directed at you, remove yourself immediately from the investigation.

It is in the interests of all parties that the defined procedure for handling grievances is followed at all times, in the spirit of fairness and with a prompt resolution of the matter.

See also

Q38   What are listening skills and why are they important?

Q56   How should I discipline team-members?

First, make a clear distinction between tackling minor disciplinary issues and addressing ongoing or unacceptable underperformance by a team-member.

For minor transgressions, adopt a coaching approach initially in an attempt to resolve the issue; in most cases, this will have a positive outcome. After all, everyone steps out of line now and again and managing these occurrences is simply part of a leader's everyday role.

However, when faced with repeated instances of improper behaviour or major deviations from acceptable norms, you may be forced to go the formal disciplinary route. Ensure that you follow whatever framework is in place in your organisation, to the letter, to avoid later legal repercussions. In addition, bear in mind these principles when taking the disciplinary route:

- Always attempt to address the matter through coaching before resorting to the formal disciplinary procedure.
- Do not attempt to rush through the disciplinary procedure; always give the employee a chance to show improvement.
- Provide the employee with an opportunity to respond to allegations and to have representation if they wish.
- Give full details of the nature of the problems to the employee.
- Remain objective throughout the process; do not pre-judge its outcome.
- Allow the employee an opportunity to appeal final decisions.

The key steps in a formal disciplinary procedure usually include:

- **Verbal warning:** After repeated violations and a failure to respond to coaching, issue the employee with a formal verbal warning that advises them of the precise nature of the problem. Also inform them that this warning represents the first stage of the disciplinary process. Explain the steps that they need to take to improve, and give a timeframe for when that improvement must be forthcoming.

Offer the employee appropriate support but be sure to inform them that failure to improve will lead to further disciplinary action. Place a record on their personnel file indicating that the verbal warning has been issued.

- **First written warning:** If the employee fails to make the necessary improvement, issue a formal written warning (some organisations provide for a second verbal warning before this stage, so check that you are following correct procedure). In this written warning, outline the problems, define what steps are necessary to demonstrate improvement and the timeframe for that improvement. Usually, this warning is disregarded for disciplinary purposes after a period defined in the warning (usually 12 months), subject to satisfactory improvement during this period.

- **Final written warning:** If the employee does not improve within the agreed timeframe, issue a final written warning, again outlining the problem and required improvements and timeframe. This warning is usually also disregarded for disciplinary purposes after a period defined in the warning, subject to satisfactory improvement during this period.

- **Dismissal or other prescribed action:** Continued failure by the employee to address the problem within the timeframe in the final written warning leads to dismissal or other appropriate sanctions.

Broadly, these are the steps to be found in any formal disciplinary procedure, although some organisations add extra tiers. Whatever you do, it is important that you follow the prescribed process and continuously involve human resources and senior managers in your decision-making.

Where an employee is considered to have committed an act of gross misconduct (usually defined as abusive or threatening behaviour, theft, bullying or sexual harassment, along with other serious offences), then you might dismiss them after a full investigation without working through the full disciplinary procedure. Often in such cases, the employee is suspended with pay until the investigation is completed. In all cases, the employee should be afforded a defined appeals mechanism against any decisions taken throughout the disciplinary process.

Clearly, the formal disciplinary route should always be the last resort and, as it is fraught with legal pitfalls, never act summarily or without consultation when applying it.

See also

Q54   How should I deal with difficult individuals in the team?

Q57   How should I respond to the high-performers in my team?

Finding and keeping high-performers is the Holy Grail in any organisation and the more of them you have on your team, the better. But they pose their own unique challenges in terms of sustaining that high performance over the long term. Surprisingly, some leaders complain about their high-performers, viewing them as demanding or, worse still, they are wary of them because they see them as a threat.

When dealing with a genuine high-performer, recognise that such individuals are usually in a hurry and often move on relatively quickly in search of new experiences. For some leaders, this makes them question why they should devote additional time to someone who will soak up the learning and move on. However, by harnessing these individuals' high motivation levels, you can benefit greatly from their presence in your team and, by increasing their levels of responsibility, delegating important work to them and involving them in decision-making, you may find that they stay with you longer because they can see the personal development opportunities that you are presenting to them.

Although you should do this with all team-members, it is critically important to agree a development plan for your high-performers, usually as an outcome from the annual performance appraisal. As part of this plan, you agree with the individual what development needs can be met in the coming year and what specific actions, including training, will be implemented. However, development plans are also a two-way street, so you want to set them challenging performance goals and targets as well. This is important because, despite being a high-performer, they are still there to do a job; they just happen to be better at it than others. Nonetheless, they still must deliver and not simply see the position as a stepping stone to something else.

In dealing with high-performing individuals, recognise the element of ego. Once they are not arrogant or condescending, this need not be a negative though it makes them challenging to lead. There is potentially a double benefit here: for you as a leader, it challenges you to be a better leader; and, through the coaching process, you can develop them, smoothing off some of their rough edges.

Be careful, though, not to treat high-performers very differently from other employees; otherwise, you will cause dissension amongst the remaining team-members. Instead, lead them in a manner that responds to their expectations and reflects their capabilities. So, for example, the high-performer is not unique in having a development plan; all that is different is what is in the plan.

Finally, note that there is a major difference between someone who is genuinely a high-performer based on their results and an individual who believes themselves to be one. If faced with the latter, do not try to 'bring them down a peg'; instead, help them develop better self-awareness as to where their strengths and areas for improvement actually lie.

See also

Q49   What makes an effective team?
Q62   Why is training and developing my employees important?

Q58   How can I deal more effectively with conflict?

Conflict is a natural feature of human interactions. In any group, clashes of personality, differences of opinions, contrasting beliefs and values or other factors can lead to conflict. With its time pressures, deadlines, and range of personalities, the workplace is the perfect environment for conflict to arise. Given its ubiquity, as a leader you need to develop your skills in resolving conflict.

No matter how good a leader you are, conflict will occur in your team from time to time. First, recognise that, although resolving conflict can be difficult, it should not be avoided; doing so simply allows it to fester and worsen. Conflict rarely dissipates without proactive action from the leader.

When you are directly in conflict with another person(s)
When considering conflict at work that involves you directly, first examine your own reactions to it. Neither aggressive nor passive behaviours will help you in such situations; when you lose control, you are no longer capable of being rational as your emotions take over. So, your first concern in conflict resolution should be to control your own emotions and reactions.

In addition, you must address the emotional aspect of the individual you are in conflict with. You need to make clear that you will listen to what they have to say, but you will not accept their overuse of emotion.

Then, it is a matter of defining the real issue and, once the problem is clear, moving towards solving it. Constant arguing over an already-identified problem is counterproductive, so you need to shift the focus to how things can be improved.

This all sounds so simple, yet you know it is not. But, if you can be calm and firm, you are well on your way to resolving conflict that directly involves you personally.

When conflict occurs between individuals in your team
In developing your ability to deal with conflict between individuals in your team (which may, or may not, involve you), it is important to accept that not all conflict is bad. Conflict can be:

- Constructive, when it leads to better ideas, or

- Destructive, when it damages relationships that are then carried into other aspects of work.

Heated debate, reasoned argument and other such forms of conflict – when focused on issues, not personalities – should be encouraged, not stifled. Passion, which is a positive force, can bring people into conflict but killing the conflict prematurely can destroy some of the passion. Your role as a leader in such circumstances is to ensure that the heat in the situation is not allowed to boil over and that the parties focus on the issue at hand. You may take a direct role in defining the solution, depending upon how the matter develops, but initially you should play a facilitation role to see whether the parties can make it through themselves. The key to handling constructive conflict is for you to control and guide the direction it takes.

A more difficult challenge is to deal with the different forms of destructive conflict that arise, which add no value in either the short or long term. Often, such conflict takes the form of personality clashes; your role here is to take direct action to resolve it.

Here are some points to consider when dealing with destructive conflict:

- Start by letting the parties involved know that you are aware of the conflict and that you are not prepared to accept it.

- Next, attempt to play a mediation role in trying to define the issues at hand and to get them to agree on a resolution.

- If necessary, meet individually with those involved and then bring them together to seek to agree on a way forward.

- If you simply tell them to stop, as is often done, this does not resolve the conflict, it just buries it, where it continues to do damage.

In some cases, you may not be able to reach a suitable resolution, particularly if it is a matter of two individuals simply disliking each other. When this happens, you must impose the required result. You cannot get them to like each other, but you can define the behaviours that you are prepared to accept from them. Then you must monitor compliance with what you have imposed. Failure to comply should have consequences, as you must send out a consistently strong message that you will not accept destructive conflict within the team.

Dealing with conflict is an everyday reality facing leaders – those who are best at resolving it have strong communication skills and, more importantly, a great understanding of people.

See also

Q27   Why is empathy important to a leader?
Q37   How can I communicate more effectively?

Q59　How should I deliver feedback for best results?

Providing feedback is something you do constantly as a leader, not just in formal situations such as appraisals and job-chats, although they too are important. Every day, as you interact with your employees, you offer feedback; sometimes, this can be job-related or, on other occasions, it may relate to aspects of the individual's behaviour and performance. Given that feedback is so integral to the leadership role, all leaders need to understand not only how best to deliver it, but some basic elements of psychology that lie behind how people cope and react to feedback.

Self-awareness and sharing

Many people lack self-awareness, so they have a limited view of their personal strengths and shortcomings; aspects of how they behave may cause difficulties for others, but they genuinely are unaware of this. Equally, most people are private to some degree and it takes time and trust before they are willing to divulge certain information to another person. It is only though developing bonds of trust with others that our willingness to open up about ourselves, and to listen to other people's opinions of us, increases.

This is vitally important for all leaders to understand. Feedback, if it is to have any value or to achieve any tangible outcomes, is dependent upon some depth of relationship existing between the giver and the receiver. Therefore, you cannot consider feedback in isolation from the wider relationships you have with your team-members. The better those bonds are, the greater the results you will achieve through giving feedback.

Delivering feedback

Even when feedback is delivered informally, there are still some general principles to adhere to because badly-delivered feedback results in no performance improvement and can damage the relationship, sometimes irreparably. So, even for *ad hoc*, informal feedback, keep the following points in mind:

- Time and place are critical when delivering individual feedback; it should never be given in front of others.

- The object of any feedback is to create awareness in the individual, so they can work towards improvement in the given area.

- The context (tone and body language) for delivering feedback is as important as the content (words) in terms of getting the employee to accept it.

- Feedback always must focus on performance, not personality, and must be directed at behaviours that potentially can be changed.

- Feedback must be based on evidence, not opinion; so, when giving feedback, you must have practical examples to support it.

- Hitting someone with a 'dose of feedback' infrequently is likely to have little impact; it should be ongoing and address issues while they are fresh.

- The aim of feedback is to help an individual to raise their performance, or change their behaviour in some way; it should always be presented in a constructive manner.

- The goal of feedback is not to tell the person the problem and the solution but rather to help them to identify their own areas for improvement and contribute to finding a solution; thus, question technique and listening skills are vital when giving feedback.

- There is no point in only focusing on positives; improvement comes from translating areas of underperformance into strengths, so negatives have to be addressed but in a helpful way.

- However, if employees only ever hear negative feedback, then they close their minds to it entirely and simply go through the motions.

- Feedback should always end on a positive note.

These basic principles are applicable in some way to all feedback activities and require you to have high levels of assertiveness, great communication skills and the ability to empathise with others.

Structuring feedback throughout the year

Employee feedback should be seen as a year-long activity combining formal and informal components, as shown:

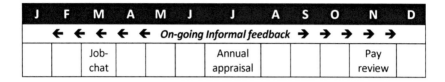

J	F	M	A	M	J	J	A	S	O	N	D
←	←	←	←	←	*On-going Informal feedback* →	→	→	→	→		
		Job-chat				Annual appraisal				Pay review	

Although these are only suggested timelines, you can see that feedback for employees has a number of elements:

- Ongoing feedback throughout the year.
- Semi-formal job-chat at the end of the first quarter.
- The formal appraisal mid-year.
- The pay review just prior to preparing the budget for the next year.

Adhering to this approach means that an employee has ample opportunities to get formal feedback on their performance. For you as leader, you can give feedback at the job-chat, then measure progress at the formal appraisal and give additional feedback, then determine how well the employee has progressed at the pay-review, which influences their pay-scale for the next year. This cycle of linked feedback is far more effective than *ad hoc* or one-off approaches and is not overly time-consuming as the job chats, annual appraisal and pay review should amount to no more than two hours per employee per year. In a large team, your assistants should be conducting some of these meetings, so logistically it is not onerous.

See also

Q20 How might I increase my self-awareness?
Q37 How can I communicate more effectively?
Q60 How can I make my performance appraisals produce better results for me?

Q60   How can I make my performance appraisals produce better results for me?

Performance appraisals – the formal evaluation of an employee's performance against defined criteria deemed relevant to their job – offer you an ideal opportunity for structured two-way communication with your team-members.

Unfortunately, some leaders waste this opportunity because they see performance appraisals as an unpleasant task, something that they are forced to do once or twice a year. Worse still, sometimes they do little with the information gathered from them. When this happens, employees quickly recognise that their leader is only going through the motions, so they too put in little effort.

Appraisals definitely must not be treated as quasi-disciplinary hearings, pay reviews, or a chance to 'tell someone what you really think of them'. Many companies combine appraisals with discussions around pay, but there is an obvious downside to that approach: do you really believe that an employee is going to be open, honest and objective about their performance during their appraisal, when they know that they will be discussing a potential pay rise at the end of it? Unlikely.

For appraisals to have real value, they must be seen in a positive light by all parties and recognised as an opportunity, not a threat. In addition, they should be viewed as discussions, not interviews as they are often called, and guided by the feedback principles outlined in **Q59**.

To help increase the effectiveness of your performance appraisals, you should consider the following three dimensions:

- Preparation.
- Conduct.
- Follow-up.

Preparation for the appraisal discussion

The key to the success of any appraisal is that both parties are prepared and fully understand what to expect. Key activities in advance of an appraisal include:

Provide the employee with advance notice	• Outline the purpose of the appraisal. • Explain / remind them how to complete the appraisal form. • Subtly guide them to reflect on specific areas if you feel there are areas for improvement for them to consider. • Agree time and location.
Review the employee's performance for the period in question	• Gather as much relevant evidence regarding the employee's performance as possible from: Previous appraisal forms / development plans; job descriptions / personnel files. • Consult with other leaders who regularly come into contact with the employee. • Review any personal objectives / goals set for them or projects the employee was involved in.
Evaluate the employee's performance	• Based on the headings on the appraisal form, you should make judgements about the employee's performance. Complete the form with your evaluation, but keep an open mind. There is no point going into the appraisal armed with 'your' result *versus* 'their' result and spending time arguing over whose appraisal is right. However, you must have some evaluation ready to guide you.
Prepare the location for the appraisal discussion	• Get the balance right between formal / informal set-up. • Allow adequate time for each appraisal. • Don't arrange too many appraisals in one day. • Make sure you will be free from disruptions. • Prepare an outline 'agenda' for discussion.

These points will ensure that both you and your team-member are prepared adequately for the session, which in turn will help to improve the result.

Conducting the appraisal

The principal aim of the appraisal is to allow discussion to take place on an employee's performance in a relaxed environment. You will have your opinion of their performance and they will have their own, but the objective is to get shared agreement as to their past performance and on how they can improve with your assistance and support. So, how you approach the session is crucial to its outcome. Use this structure:

Introduction	• Welcome. • Break the ice. • Restate purpose, format, time, their / your role. • Emphasise objective.
Review performance	• Encourage the employee to review their overall performance since the last job-chat / appraisal. • Use question technique and listening skills to get them to open up. • Praise performance, where appropriate. • Then review specific performance under each appraisal heading. • Seek their opinion first. • Discuss strengths / weaknesses. • Give feedback on their performance in that area. • Agree result / rating last. Do not allow the discussion to turn into "I gave you 3 for that, what did you rate yourself?". That is pointless. Discuss the performance, then agree the rating.
Identify areas for improvement	• Discuss in detail the causes of performance weaknesses identified. • Seek their opinions on how they can improve. • Identify training and development needs. • Use question technique and listening skills.
Agree action	• Discuss how to maintain their strengths. • Agree action required to help them to improve weak areas. • Set personal objectives and agree their development plan for the next period. • Gain their commitment to what is agreed.
Close session	• Summarise the key points. • Outline the follow-up. • Explain what happens with the appraisal form. • Thank them.

Following-up the appraisal

Once the appraisal session is over, you should:

- Complete the agreed appraisal form.
- Record action points.
- Complete any administration.
- Follow-up.

If you take these principles and structure on board, you will find that you get enhanced outcomes from your appraisals in future.

A key point to remember is that you want the employee, as far as is possible, to identify their own strengths and areas for improvement. Most people respond well to appraisals when you do your job correctly in both preparing for, and delivering, them.

See also

Q59 How should I deliver feedback for best results?

Q61   How should I recognise and reward my employees?

Usually when the issue of recognising and rewarding employees is raised, thoughts immediately turn to monetary compensation. While pay is a factor here, it is not the only avenue available to you when it comes to acknowledging the efforts of your team. Beyond pay and conditions, there are plenty of options open to you in terms of recognising and rewarding your people, ranging from a simple "thank you" to providing some form of employee recognition scheme. Examples include:

- **Saying "Thank You":** Do not underestimate the power of thanking your team, individually and collectively, when they deliver for you. In addition to thanking an individual directly when they excel, explore how you can acknowledge their efforts publicly through employee notice boards, company newsletters and so on.

- **Training and development as a reward:** Although it depends on the individual, rewarding high performance through further training and development opportunities should not be overlooked.

- **Vouchers and discounts:** Liaise with your suppliers for vouchers or discounts to offer to employees when they achieve beyond expectations.

- **Recognition schemes:** When employee recognition schemes are well-structured, seen to be objective and based on some discernable and measureable criteria, they can be worthwhile. If your organisation does not have a scheme, develop an informal scheme within your department, or the part of the organisation for which you are responsible. If you do so:
  - Define specific criteria upon which the award is to be based. Often employees are nominated for recognition on subjective grounds. Your approach needs to be more rigorous and transparent than that; how can an employee strive to win the award, if they don't know what criteria it is based on?

- Agree how often the award will be made, how that decision will be taken and who will be involved in selecting the winner against the agreed criteria.
- Identify how the winner will be recognised and whether there will be an overall winner each year from those who won a monthly or quarterly award.
- Make the award attractive – is it something that people would strive to achieve?

An added benefit of an informal, but well-managed, recognition scheme is that it allows you to promote certain values and behaviours through the criteria that you develop around the award.

These are only samples of the many things you can do to recognise and reward your team-members. The only limitation on what else might be done is your propensity for creativity.

See also

Q52 How can I motivate and engage my team-members better?
Q62 Why is training and developing my employees important?

Q62   Why is training and developing my employees important?

Training and development is critical in terms of raising individual and collective performance. To get the best outcomes from training and development, view it as an investment and, just as you would for any investment, seek to maximise the return it gives you. This mindset will help you to plan, deliver and measure better the impact of the training and development you provide for your team-members.

Often the difference between training and development is unclear and, although the two go hand-in-hand, there are subtle distinctions between them. Training tends to focus on the skills and knowledge an individual requires to be effective in their current role; it can be delivered both on and off-the-job; it has a more immediate focus and is intended to balance the needs of the organisation with those of the individual. Development, on the other hand, tends to focus on the employee's future, looking at how the organisation can help them to progress and develop, examining more closely their individual motivations, aspirations and potential. In other words, development looks at the bigger picture and takes a longer-term view.

Key considerations in relation to training and development
The most important function of training and development is to raise individual and collective competence so that better outcomes are achieved. This is good for the organisation and, if the training is well-designed and delivered, this is good for the individual too. As a leader, you naturally want your people to be competent at what they do – but you also should want all employees on the same level to be similarly capable, with everyone achieving a minimum level of competence. When some people are less competent, others in the team have to compensate for them and, over the long term, this causes potential for frustration and resentment. So, apart from the obvious need for training and development in relation to the quality of outcomes, it also has an impact on team harmony.

Training and development should always be structured:

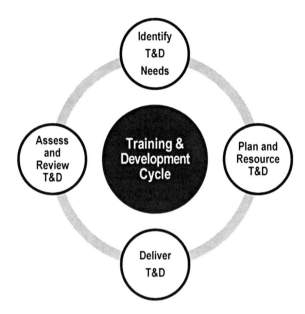

Unless all training provided follows this cycle, then it is likely to prove less effective than it might otherwise be. Reflect on these important points:

- In *identifying training and development needs*, you need to consider both the requirements of the organisation and, by using the information gained from performance appraisals and other sources, the specific needs of the individual.

- When all training and development needs are identified, they should to be *planned* and budgeted for. Although you may have budget constraints, it is more effective to define all the training and development that should be done first, and then to decide what can be done based on the resources available.

- The *delivery of training and development* must be stimulating and engaging for your employees, so you need to consider who delivers it, and how good they are at doing so – this applies equally to internal trainers and external consultants. Badly-delivered training – whatever the source and / or however cheap – is a waste of time.

- *Assessing and reviewing* training and development is critical, for it is only by doing so that you can measure your return on investment. Admittedly, it is not always easy to quantify outcomes, which might include, for example, increased customer or employee satisfaction, revenue growth or cost reduction. But it is vital that you link the provision of training with results and that you have the systems in place to provide you with the data required to measure its impact.

By considering these four elements in the training and development cycle, you will see a better return on investment over the long term.

See also

Q52   How can I motivate and engage my team-members better?
Q63   How should I coach my employees to improved performance?

Q63   How should I coach my employees to improved performance?

Coaching is linked inextricably to training and development in that it has to do with helping employees raise their performance. There are two types of coaching:

- Corrective coaching.
- Performance coaching.

Corrective coaching relates to situations where an employee is struggling with a particular task or skill in their job; the willingness and motivation is there but they are having some problems getting it right. They do not need formal training as such, but need help to get that final piece of the puzzle in place.

Performance coaching, on the other hand, is broader in scope and seeks to resolve attitudinal and behavioural issues that affect an individual's results. Thus, it is a greater challenge for leaders.

Performance coaching can take place in a variety of scenarios, ranging from a directive approach by the leader to one of facilitation:

Problem identified by	Leader	Leader	Employee	Employee
Solution identified by	Leader	Employee	Leader	Employee
Approach	Directive ➔ ➔	➔ ➔	➔ ➔	Facilitative

Depending upon the issue, and indeed the employee involved, you may be forced to be directive in terms of how you coach others; if they refuse to respond to your efforts, you map out the problem for them and also determine the solution. Clearly, this approach has limitations, as the employee takes no ownership for the situation. At the other end of the scale, you operate in full coach mode, using your skills to help the employee to both define the problem and the solution. This is a preferred approach, as the employee essentially directs their own development, but it takes a lot of skill as a leader to be able to draw out the problem and then guide the employee to define the solution. In between these two extremes are situations where the employee might raise a problem with you and you offer guidance on the solution, or where you raise the issue but lead them towards defining the best way forward.

Regardless of which coaching scenario is involved, keep the following points in mind:

- Simply telling a difficult or underperforming employee to change their attitude or behaviour is likely to have limited impact because, in most instances, they do not think there is a problem in the first place – more likely they believe it is you who has the problem.

- For that reason, the first goal of performance coaching is to get the employee to accept that there is an issue to be addressed. They may do so readily on their own, but more often than not, you will have to coach them towards that acceptance.

- When operating in coach mode, your ability to remain calm and in control is vital. Some difficult employees know exactly which buttons to press and, if you react, then not only will the coaching fail, but you will give them the pleasure of having wound you up.

- The ability to use all your communication skills to good effect – question technique, listening skills, managing tone and body language – lies at the heart of being an effective coach.

- When faced with a significant attitudinal or behavioural problem, recognise that you need to be realistic about your goals in terms of outcomes. It is unlikely you will see a radical turnaround from a single coaching session but, if you see progress in the right direction, that is an achievement in itself. It usually takes a number of attempts to get to your ultimate goal.

Recognise that performance coaching is only applicable in situations where the employee has some value within the team. Everyone has attitudinal or behavioural issues, at times, that they need to be taken to task over; performance coaching is intended for that purpose. However, for a negative employee who is a continuous disruptive influence, performance coaching is unlikely to have any effect, so you need to question whether it is a worthwhile investment of your time. Equally, if any employee fails to respond to your coaching efforts, then you are likely heading towards the disciplinary route with them. The best leaders attempt to coach first, then discipline, but only if the coaching fails to deliver the desired result.

See also

Q37 How can I communicate more effectively?
Q56 How should I discipline team-members?
Q62 Why is training and developing my employees important?

Q64   Is counselling my employees something I should be doing?

Leaders are frequently concerned where the boundaries lie between coaching and counselling and, no matter how experienced you are in leading others, there are always important issues to be considered here. In simple terms, coaching addresses work-related attitudinal or behavioural problems that impact directly on an individual's performance, whereas counselling involves coping with personal problems that cause an employee to underperform. Obviously, the lines between these two can blur, giving rise to a challenge for all leaders.

On the one hand, for you to become the best leader that you can be, you must take some level of personal interest in your employees; you cannot remain totally aloof from them as individuals, for to do so is not to lead. However, you also have to weigh that objective against the potential danger of allowing your relationships with your team-members to develop so that you end up serving as some form of mother-hen. It is a matter of knowing where to draw the line – and there are no precise rules to guide you, only commonsense.

The need to counsel your employees can arise in many ways. For example, often through the informal and formal coaching of team-members, issues emerge that are not directly work-related, but impact on how they perform. You cannot ignore such issues. Equally, when you have strong bonds between a leader and their team, some employees may approach the leader about personal matters that have nothing at all to do with work. In either of these situations, if you are serious about leadership, you cannot ignore the fact that you are faced with counselling. However, it is how you do so that really matters.

First, your role always should be to listen to the individual, showing support and empathy for them and their predicament. If it is a matter that significantly affects their work performance, you must get them to recognise that they need to find a solution because you cannot overlook underperformance indefinitely. Of course, and particularly for normally high-performing employees, you are prepared to be as flexible as you can and will endeavour to give them time and space to deal with the matter, but that can only ever be a short-term solution. So, even though you are supportive, you also must get the message across subtly that the focus has to be on finding a solution.

As you show this supportive side, though, you should be very clear that your role is not to counsel them on the specific issue at hand. If it is a serious matter, you probably are not qualified to give advice but, even if you feel you can, it is still better not to do so because, if that advice turns out to be wrong, then it can all backfire on you.

This is the correct line to take with regard to your role as a leader in terms of counselling. You empathise, but you do not get directly involved in the matter. You should help them to identify where they can get the necessary help and guidance they need. You do not abdicate your responsibilities by doing this but you should never recommend a particular course of action or suggest someone they should 'go and see'; usually the appropriate advice is to convince them to speak with someone in human resources who can steer them in the right direction.

See also

Q63 How should I coach my employees to improved performance?

Q65   What is empowerment and how much autonomy should I give my employees?

Empowerment means that the leader releases the reins of control to allow employees a greater degree of freedom or autonomy over how they do their work. At a low level, employees might be empowered to deal with customers in a certain way; for example, they may be able to make on-the-spot decisions as to how to reimburse a customer when a complaint arises. But, this form of empowerment is only the tip of the iceberg; true empowerment means treating employees as genuine partners, involving them fully in decision-making and allowing them to take greater ownership for how they do their own work.

Empowering employees is good for leaders because it brings out the best in their team-members. However, do not think of it as a gift within your power to bestow because, more and more today, employees expect to be empowered. Employees increasingly are less inclined to engage fully in jobs where they are treated as implementers without any input into the decision-making process itself.

The extent to which you empower your employees is determined by:

- **Organisational culture:** The culture of the organisation within which you work naturally plays a significant role in determining the degree to which you can empower your people; either the culture and, as a result, the policies and procedures facilitate the empowerment of employees or restrain your efforts.

- **Leader readiness:** How comfortable are you in releasing control? If you are a 'control freak', then you simply will not be comfortable in empowering your people – but you will suffer for it in the long run.

- **Employee readiness:** How effective are your employees, individually and collectively as a team? Yet, if you never empower them, then they never become ready to be further empowered.

- **Nature of the work:** A customer-facing environment is ideal territory for empowering your people, as they are in direct contact with clients and it is better that they can make immediate decisions.

In contrast, if you are involved in dangerous or highly technical work, there may be less scope for empowerment in doing the actual work, though your people may be empowered in other ways.

If there is very little empowerment at present, start small and work towards more substantial empowerment over the longer term. Some initial steps you might take include:

- **Encourage your employees to become more involved in decision-making:** Put teams together, identify a problem and ask them to consider potential solutions. There is no danger for you as a leader in doing this, once you guide them on the parameters within which any solution must fit. Over time, you will find that they will come to you with solutions for problems without you having to ask.

- **Encourage ideas and suggestions:** Create a mechanism that facilitates your employees in making ideas and suggestions. Define key categories to guide their ideas – increase customer satisfaction, improve teamwork, reduce costs and so on.

- **Allow them to take decisions:** If you are in a customer-facing environment, identify with your team-members areas that currently require your decision and explore what authority can be passed to them, within specified boundaries.

- **Get them to participate more:** For example, instead of you chairing the weekly team meeting, allow each employee to take charge on a rota basis.

In deciding what you can do with your team, think about where they are in terms of effectiveness. With an ineffective team, you can only take tiny steps in terms of empowerment; with an effective team, there already should be a lot of empowerment in place and you can do more; with an excelling team, they already should be very highly empowered.

See also

Q50   How do teams change and develop over time?
Q51   What is the difference between organisation culture and climate?
Q52   How can I motivate and engage my team-members better?

Q66   How should I manage employee diversity effectively?

You should embrace diversity, in all its forms; the more diverse your team, the better. At the same time, recognise that diversity brings with it many challenges for you as a leader. For the most part, the basic principles of how to lead others apply regardless of who is involved, but they are not always the same when different cultures are involved.

Your organisation already may have formal diversity policies in place and, if so, you must be guided by what is stipulated in them. In general, your role as leader in this area is to:

- Constantly build your own knowledge and understanding of different perspectives, cultures and the needs of the disabled.
- Set the benchmark for others in terms of how you embrace diversity.
- Ensure that diversity awareness underpins all your efforts as a leader.
- Prevent any form of discrimination from taking place within your team.
- Challenge and change practices and procedures that restrict your efforts to manage diversity.

Practical measures you can put in place within your team to support the management of diversity include:

- Get to know all members of your team so that you understand their beliefs, expectations and motivations better.
- Have a clear plan as to how you will pro-actively manage diversity within your team. Do not leave it to chance.
- Ensure that diversity awareness training is provided for all and, in particular, forms part of the employee induction.

- Use your ongoing coaching and feedback sessions to help develop individual self-awareness, in terms of understanding their own culture, biases, prejudices, and stereotypes.

- Be open with your team about diversity. Discuss the matter regularly with them.

- Identify team goals in relation to diversity, then get your team-members to agree clear principles and actions that will help make those goals a reality.

- Ensure that you allow equal opportunities in the recruitment, selection and promotion of your employees.

- Ensure that suggestions on how to improve diversity management is included as a heading on your employee suggestion form.

- Consider celebrating national days within your team, whereby individuals from different countries can celebrate and also teach others about their culture.

- Never allow any form of bullying or discrimination to go unchallenged.

- Maximise the use of team-based initiatives and ensure that the diversity of the team as a whole is reflected in those sub-teams.

Finally, do not manage diversity with the mindset that it is a chore but, instead, recognise that a more diverse team is potentially a better team, as it brings a range of attributes, talents and perspectives not seen in a more homogenous group.

See also

Q72 Why is new employee induction so important to maintaining a positive team dynamic?

Q67   How should I retain my best employees?

How to keep your best people is a concern for all leaders and, as with most aspects of leading others, there are no magic answers. Employees come and go, but you always should be aware of how the rate of employee turnover in your team compares not only with other departments within the organisation but with comparable organisations. If your rate of employee turnover is worse than the norm, then you should pay particular attention to this area because, apart from the cost, it is an indicator that you may be doing something wrong in terms of how you lead people.

A second consideration relates to who you consider to be your 'best' employees. On the one hand, you must accept that high-performers will always move on in search of new opportunities, so the best you can do is to prolong their stay. But being a great employee does not always mean being the most talented; you probably have team-members who lack the high-performers' ambition but are vital contributors, whom you want to keep. So, a fundamental requirement in relation to retaining employees is to know what makes them tick, so that you can tailor your response.

At a macro-level, organisational culture and pay and conditions play an important part in employee retention. If you have responsibility for them, you must ensure they serve to retain, not repulse, people. Factors that influence retention, which are within the direct control of all leaders, include:

- **How you lead your employees:** People work for other people, not for organisations. One of the most common reasons cited in feedback surveys by employees who leave jobs is dissatisfaction with their immediate boss. Working as hard as you can to build your skills as a leader, of itself, makes a big contribution to the retention of employees.

- **How you recruit your people:** Unless you recruit the right people, you will have a higher turnover rate. And, unless you really try to understand a potential employee's motivations during the recruitment process, you are likely to take people onboard with false expectations, which will make it harder to retain them.

- **How empowered they feel:** Another major problem frequently highlighted as a key reason for changing a job is feeling over-controlled or micro-managed. Employees who do not feel empowered, particularly the talented ones, are unlikely to stay with you for any longer than they must to achieve their own objectives.

- **How valued they feel:** Unless you have a range of measures in place to reward and recognise your employees, you run the risk of making them feel undervalued. Obviously, this may drive some of them elsewhere in search of the recognition they feel they deserve.

- **How they are growing as individuals:** None of us want to feel that we are standing still in life and, in the absence of structured development opportunities, many employees will grow disgruntled with their present employer.

Of course, issues such as career paths, pay-scales and overall organisation culture play a direct role on retention levels but these points above are directly within your control.

See also

Q35   What are the core leadership skills that contribute to success?
Q62   Why is training and developing my employees important?
Q65   What is empowerment and how much should I give my employees?
Q69   What should I look for when I recruit new team-members?
Q91   Why is succession planning important?

Q68   Why are exit interviews important?

Employee feedback is always useful to help leaders learn and improve. It is particularly valuable when obtained from employees who are leaving. For the most part, employees who are departing on positive terms have no axe to grind and can be open and objective about their experiences. A good exit interview process can help you to diagnose your strengths and areas for improvement as a leader, as well as give you insights into a range of issues that may be impacting on employee satisfaction or retention.

As well as providing you as a leader with useful feedback, an effective exit interview with a departing employee can help to identify information that is useful to remaining employees. Especially in sales or customer relationship management roles, departing employees may have insights that others in the team may lack. Of course, there should be a handover process anyway, but the exit interview provides an additional one-on-one opportunity to pick up on any points that may have been overlooked. You cannot force the leaver to divulge their personal know-how but you have a better chance of finding it out by asking than if you never ask at all.

Structured exit interviews can:

- Enhance your understanding of how effective you are at leading others.
- Provide wider information that can help to improve the working environment within the organisation.
- Retain know-how that might otherwise be lost.
- Deliver insights on improving employee retention.
- Help you to find out what other organisations are offering to attract employees that you may not be doing.
- Create a lasting and positive impression on the departing employee.

Apart from asking general questions as to why they are leaving, and seeking to retain any know-how they might be willing to discuss, also ask specific questions such as:

- How well did your experience with us live up to promises made during the recruitment process?
- How well did you feel you were led during your time with us?
- How did the training and development opportunities provided to you live up to your expectations? Where were the gaps?
- How empowered did you feel working here?
- What aspects of how you were recognised for your work made you feel valued? What suggestions might you have to improve on this?
- How effective did you feel communication was within the team? Between teams? How do you think this might be improved?
- How would you describe the working conditions here generally?
- What could we have done to make you stay with us?

When an employee leaves on a high note, this might influence future career decisions they take and you may find some of them seeking to rejoin the organisation at a later stage or recommending it to others, so in this sense the exit interview has a public relations component to it as well.

See also

Q20   How might I increase my self-awareness?
Q67   How should I retain my best employees?

Q69 What should I look for when I recruit new team-members?

As a leader, you should pay a lot of attention to the people you bring into your team. Selecting the right person for the job can make a major positive contribution to building the overall effectiveness of your team; get it wrong and you can cause serious damage to morale. You also should recognise that it is always easier to keep a 'bad egg' out than it is to get rid of them once they have joined – and add to this the wasted costs of having to begin the search all over again.

Although many organisations now use job descriptions and employee profiles to aid the recruitment process, some leaders do not make best use of them and still place too much emphasis on gut feeling, which is a factor, but should not form the majority component of any recruitment decision. In seeking any new employee, you need to think about three dimensions:

Background / experience	Skills / knowledge	Personal attributes
What *education or training qualifications* do you expect the ideal candidate to have to be able to do the job?	What specific *skills and knowledge* must they have already to do the job to the standard you require?	What overall *personality / disposition* are you looking for in the person?
What level of *work experience* are you looking for?	What *communication skills* do they require?	What *personal attributes* must they have? *Define them very clearly.*

Generally, you can determine what a candidate can do by analysing their CV or by looking at the past jobs they have held but determining who they are – whether they are the right candidate – in terms of attitude and behaviour is far more challenging. As you well know, candidates are likely to tell you what you want to hear at interviews, but whether that is the whole truth is sometimes another matter. To avoid this pitfall, profile an ideal candidate and then benchmark all potential applicants against that profile. Using the profile, devise a range of questions designed to draw out the information you require, with particular emphasis on the personal qualities you are looking for. For example, if you are looking for a team-player, asking a candidate whether they are a team-player is unlikely to yield anything but a 'Yes' answer. So your questions must be better thought through than that, perhaps along these lines:

- Give me some examples of where you felt you made a positive contribution to your team in the past?

- What do you think your previous team-mates would say about working with you?

- What can you bring to our team that would set you apart from other candidates?

It is only by having a clear picture in your mind of what you are looking for that you can hope to find the best candidate from a pool of applicants. Otherwise, the interview process normally works like this: the first candidate sets the benchmark; the second is either better or worse; and so on down the line. Thus, the interviewer does no more than compare one candidate against another, which allows them to be swayed by those who 'do a good interview'. The approach described here prevents this from happening.

See also

Q70 How can I use the interview process better to help me find the best people for my team?

Q71 What other tools can I use to help me select the best employees?

Q70   How can I use the interview process more effectively to help me find the best people for my team?

Although fraught with shortcomings, interviews remain a core element of the recruitment process in most organisations, albeit frequently supplemented by psychometric tests and other analytical tools. The biggest problem with interviews is not the interview itself, but the limitations of those conducting them; many people are simply bad interviewers. You can enhance your ability to find the right candidate more often using interviews simply by improving your skills at it.

Some tips in this regard include:

- Always prepare fully for interviews in advance. Assess the CV / application before the interview, not during it. Reading through a candidate's CV for the first time during the interview is bad practice.
- Prepare the interview area in advance. Choose a private setting, not too formal, where you and the candidate can both concentrate.
- Prepare an interview plan, incorporating your structured questions based on the profile you developed for the ideal candidate.
- Try not to make your judgement too early. Research shows that many interviewers make up their mind within the first few minutes and then subconsciously adjust the interview accordingly.
- Use an effective question technique, avoiding closed questions that enable candidates to give yes / no answers.
- Follow an interview plan, asking all candidates the same or similar questions. This is the only way to compare like with like.
- Ensure that your questions probe who the candidate really is so that you get behind the standard rehearsed answers.
- Use two interviewers or a second interview, where possible, as you get a more rounded view.
- Limit the number of candidates you see in any one day so that you stay fresh and alert for all candidates.

These general considerations will go a long way in helping you to improve the quality of the people you select. In addition, use this well-known structure for holding an interview (WASP):

- **Welcome:** During this initial phase, you should:
    - Establish rapport and break the ice, as a relaxed candidate will perform better.
    - Explain the purpose of the interview.
    - Outline the format for the interview with approximate timings.
    - Inform the candidate that you will be taking notes.

- **Acquire Information:** In this phase, seek to get as many relevant (and that is a key word) details from the candidate as possible, so that you can make an informed decision about their suitability:
    - Begin with general questions, moving to the more specific.
    - Use your question technique to explore background, attitudes, suitability, etc. relevant to the employee profile you are seeking.
    - Probe to explore any 'gaps' – but do not interrogate the candidate.
    - Let the candidate speak, use your listening skills. Do not forget the 80/20 rule; they should be talking for 80% of the time, not you.

    This phase of the interview, in terms of timing, should form the main component. Remember that, as you assess the candidate, they are also assessing you and making judgements about you and the organisation, so you want to come across as highly professional.

- **Supply information:** Once you have obtained all the relevant information you need, allow the candidate to ask you questions about the position. You should ensure that you:
    - Outline the job description in greater detail, giving an overview of their potential role in the company.
    - Provide the candidate with details on the salary and conditions associated with the position.
    - Answer any remaining questions.

- **Plan and part:** The final section of the interview is designed to ensure that both parties leave the interview fully aware of the next steps in the selection process. During this phase, you should:
    - Ask to check references.

- Discuss salary if not mentioned already.
- Give a timetable for the decision and how they will be notified.
- Thank them.

In some cases, you may wish to provide the candidate with a tour of your facilities; this can be done at this stage. Once a candidate leaves, allow time before the next applicant to review their performance and to prepare a written evaluation and rating against the defined criteria. By doing so, at the end of the day's interviewing, you will have a set of evaluations and will be able to identify the higher-scoring candidates.

Having structure and, more importantly, the right technique will increase the effectiveness of your interviews.

See also

Q71   What other tools can I use to help me select the best employees?

Many organisations enhance the recruitment process, to help ensure that they choose the best available candidate, by using tools such as assessment centres, presentations and psychometric tests to better evaluate the applicants. The tools available to you naturally depend upon the practices adopted by your organisation, but you can adopt some of the principles described here to strengthen how you select your employees.

Assessment centres have grown in popularity, particularly for senior level recruitment. Usually, they consist of a full-day event where candidates are presented with a number of structured assessment activities designed to really test their motivation and suitability for the post. These events often take place at the later stages of the recruitment process when the broad field of candidates has been narrowed down, so they can be quite intense and competitive; but that too is part of the rationale for using them. The events may involve a combination of activities, including:

- Psychometric tests.
- Individual / group exercises.
- Case study analysis.
- Formal presentations.
- Role plays.
- Behavioural interviews.

By providing for a more detailed exploration of a candidate's suitability, assessment centres have been proven to be a more effective method of selection. Clearly, organising and managing an assessment centre takes time, money and expertise but, if they result in better recruitment decisions, then they represent a good return on investment.

Even if you are not in a position to devote the necessary resources towards running a full assessment centre, you might use some of the tools individually:

- **Psychometric tests:** Psychometric tests are designed to assess an individual's reasoning abilities or to gauge their likely behavioural responses to a variety of situations. By testing a candidate in these areas, you can compare their score to accepted norms; the results can support the decision-making process during recruitment. Generally, you will come across two main types of tests:
    - Ability tests seek to measure a candidate's skills in areas such as numeracy, verbal reasoning, analytical capabilities and so on. They are frequently conducted under time constraints, so they can also demonstrate how well an individual can cope under pressure.
    - Personality questionnaires, on the other hand, can be used to evaluate a candidate's likely behaviour and attitudes according to a variety of situations, such as their ability to interact with other team-members or how they might deal with a range of work based scenarios.

- **Role plays / presentations / group exercises:** Integrating role plays, presentations and exercises into your recruitment process can be particularly suitable when seeking to fill sales or customer-facing positions. For example, if you had a large number of applicants for a particular post, bringing them together and setting them an exercise to work upon in groups, while monitoring their performance, could help in 'screening' candidates to ensure that you only interview those with the greatest potential. Equally, having a sales candidate make a short presentation as part of the interview process makes good sense, as you want to see how they can communicate to potential clients.

- **Behavioural interviewing:** You always should ensure that the majority of your questions posed during the interview have a behavioural component to them, which are linked to the employee profile you are searching for. This can be achieved simply by presenting candidates with scenarios related to the role and asking them to explain how they would deal with the situation.

A further addition that you could consider to enhance your recruitment efforts is to ask potential candidates to work with your team for a short period, so that you can judge better how they perform on-site and whether they integrate well with your team. In fact, in some organisations, the existing team members are involved in making the final decision on recruitment. This approach is becoming more popular and, as candidates are paid for their time, they are not being treated unfairly. However, you only can do this if you have a high-performing team and, indeed, if your organisation is open to this approach.

See also

Q69 What should I look for when I recruit new team-members?
Q70 How can I use the interview process better to help me find the best people for my team?

Q72   Why is new employee induction so important to maintaining a positive team dynamic?

You do not get a second chance to make a good first impression when it comes to a new employee. Yet, it is amazing how often new team-members are thrown in at the deep end with little or no formal induction training or support. You should avoid this, because the benefits of a solid induction far outweigh the time and effort required to deliver it. Recognise also that most employees start with high potential for engagement, but this can quickly evaporate if their introduction to your team is poor. Equally, a bad start in an organisation can result in the time and expense invested in the recruitment process being wasted.

An employee's induction should involve the following components:

- **An introduction to the organisation:** This is where the employee is given an overview of the business, its vision and mission and the broader picture of what it means to work there. If you are a senior leader in your organisation, you should ensure that the induction of new employees helps to build their understanding of, and commitment to, what you are striving to achieve. Apart from the various legal requirements that employees are entitled to receive at the outset, such as contracts and so on, this introduction to the organisation is a critical first opportunity to really engage the employee with the organisation and the people working there.

- **An introduction to their department:** As well as an overall induction to the business, each employee should receive a detailed introduction to the specific area where they will be working. It is this aspect of induction that often falls short of requirements. If you are a leader at this level, recognise that this is your best opportunity to help the new employee understand your personal vision and what you expect of them in terms of their attitude, behaviour and overall performance and be prepared to spend time with them. As part of this phase of their induction, the employee should receive a clear outline of their job description and other operational aspects of their role. These more mundane aspects of the induction can be covered by your assistants but it is critical that new recruits get the bigger picture from you.

If you do not provide your new team-members with a full induction, then somebody else probably will and you can be sure that it will be the one or two negative or frustrated employees who get to them first because they are always on the lookout for new recruits to the 'cheesed-off club'.

See also

Q69 What should I look for when I recruit new team-members?
Q73 How should I monitor a new employee's performance?

Q73 How should I monitor a new employee's performance?

Most employees are given some form of probation period when they join an organisation, usually three or six months. It is vital that you ensure that their performance is monitored and reviewed at defined intervals within that period. Otherwise, bad habits can set in or, even worse, you can miss clear signals of underperformance, which are infinitely more difficult to resolve once the individual has been accepted as a full-time employee and has acquired additional employment rights. In addition, when you believe you have found the right employee, which you clearly do at this point, you should want to make sure that their first few months enhance their experience, not devalue their impression of working for you.

Key milestones for a new employee include:

- At the end of their **first day**, devote a moment or two to check with the employee to see how they are feeling. It is likely to be too early for them, or you, to have much to discuss but it shows them from the outset that you are concerned they settle in well.

- At the end of their **first week**, have a chat with them about their experience so far. This can help to highlight any issues that, if left unattended, could create unnecessary problems.

- At the end of the **first month**, have a more formal meeting with the employee to review their performance in greater detail. By this time, they should have completed all their initial training and you will have had enough time to evaluate how well they are performing and, equally important, how they are fitting in with the remainder of the team. As part of this discussion, you can:
  - Get their feedback on how they are feeling and identify any blockages.
  - Highlight for them any issues of concern you may have as regards their performance.
  - Define additional areas where you feel further training or coaching is required.

If, by this time, a candidate has fallen well below expectations, you need to be very clear as to what those problems are, what they need to do to address them and you should establish timeframes when you will meet with them again to review their progress.

In some organisations, new employees receive little or no feedback during their probation period, only to be told near the end of it that "things have not worked out" as expected. Apart from this being unfair on the individual concerned, by not providing ongoing, structured feedback there is potential that an underperforming employee can have a negative influence on the team and, even though they leave, you will possibly be left with some residual problems to address because of the destructive influence they had while with your organisation.

See also

Q59   How should I deliver feedback for best results?
Q72   Why is new employee induction so important to maintaining a positive team dynamic?

Q74   Should I socialise with my team?

This may appear a trivial question but it is raised frequently by leaders, both young and experienced. On the one hand, you do not want to be too distant from your people; on the other, socialising with them brings with it potential pitfalls.

When handled well, spending time socialising with your employees can be a positive thing to do, because it gives them a chance to interact with you on a less formal level. It can be a time to let them see a different side to you and it can also be useful for you to see how the dynamic of the team functions away from the workplace. Indeed, it should simply be a time to have fun.

Problems can arise, however, if you do not maintain some boundaries in such circumstances, especially if the outing involves a night in the pub, since alcohol has the potential to create problems for you in a number of ways. Some employees, emboldened by a few beers, may feel that it is the appropriate time to tell you a few home truths; others may view it as a chance to catch the boss off-guard, so be careful in such situations not to speak out-of-turn about work-related matters.

Socialising with your team is not something you should completely avoid. It is a good thing to do, on occasion, if you follow some commonsense principles. Go along, have a laugh, keep the conversation light and head for the door before things get messy.

See also

Q11   What do employees look for in a leader?

KEY LEADERSHIP ACTIVITIES

Q75   How do I achieve excellence in my organisation?

Today, you hear the term 'excellence' widely used in all organisations, in all fields of business; everything is about excellence now, or so it seems. Yet, for all its widespread use, excellence remains an obscure concept even to define – for everyone's view of it varies – let alone achieve.

Excellence means striving to become a leading organisation within whatever field you operate and doing so with measurable evidence to demonstrate you are achieving that goal. The diagram below summarises the elements involved:

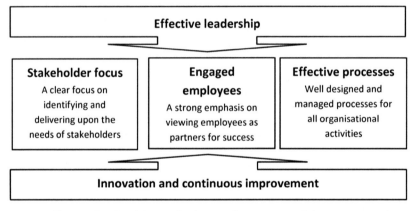

Effective leadership

Stakeholder focus	Engaged employees	Effective processes
A clear focus on identifying and delivering upon the needs of stakeholders	A strong emphasis on viewing employees as partners for success	Well designed and managed processes for all organisational activities

Innovation and continuous improvement

- **Effective leadership:** At the heart of any successful organisation lies effective leadership, at every level from the CEO to the warehouse supervisor. In terms of driving excellence, senior leaders must define what it means in practice and communicate it through the vision, mission and strategic goals. Next, they develop strategies and plans to achieve excellence and compare results externally to demonstrate that the organisation is excelling in comparison to its peers. Effective leadership also means that all leaders are aware of, and committed to, the agreed direction for the organisation and they work collectively to create and sustain a culture that supports the drive for excellence. It involves leading by example every day.

- **Stakeholder focus:** Achieving excellence means continuously being pro-active in understanding, and responding to, the needs of key stakeholders who, depending upon the organisation, can be customers, employees, suppliers, investors and / or the wider community. Excellent organisations do not pay lip service in this regard, but have defined structures in place that allow them to stay closely in tune with their stakeholders' needs and that also facilitate the measurement of their success at meeting those needs.

- **Engaged employees:** Little on any journey to excellence can be achieved without engaged employees, because all the aspirations in the world are meaningless unless those who do the work actually believe in what they are doing and are committed to being the best.

- **Effective processes:** Every function within the organisation contributes in some way to the achievement of excellence, so all processes must be designed and managed in such a way as to help, not hinder, that effort.

- **Innovation and continuous improvement:** Excellence is a journey, guided by:
  - Constantly measuring organisation performance against competitors and best-in-class organisations.
  - Learning the lessons and identifying best practices.
  - Adapting those best practices and applying them in context.

  Organisations that excel are always results-driven, strive constantly to raise the bar and innovate continuously to ensure that they retain their leadership position.

Without these fundamental drivers in place, achieving excellence remains but a dream.

See also

Q16   What personal attributes are required to be a successful leader?
Q35   What are the core leadership skills that contribute to success?
Q52   How can I motivate and engage my team-members better?
Q96   How can I encourage and manage innovation?

Q76   What is the strategic planning process?

An important element in achieving excellence is the strategic planning process, whereby an overall direction for the organisation is established by its leaders. Once upon a time, strategic planning was considered to have a long-term (that is, 10 years) horizon but, with increased volatility in the business environment, strategic planning today generally means a three to five-year window.

Key elements of the process include:

It is important to view strategic planning as a continuous process, rather than as something done at defined intervals. At any given time, leaders should be focusing on some activity related to the overall strategic planning process.

Nor is it a step-by-step process, where each step follows directly after the other. For example, in the diagram above, the key activities from developing vision, mission and values to agreeing strategy are very much interlinked and often can be addressed in unison over a given period of time.

See also

Q77   Why are organisational vision, mission and values important?
Q78   How should vision, mission and values be developed?
Q79   How should vision, mission and values be used for best effect?
Q80   What analysis is important when strategic planning?
Q82   How should I develop and implement strategy?
Q83   How can I review strategic effectiveness?

Q77   Why are organisational vision, mission and values important?

The concepts of vision, mission and values get a lot of negative publicity these days and rightly so, because they are widely misused in how they are developed and, more importantly, applied within many organisations. All too frequently, flowery but meaningless vision, mission and values statements are developed, designed more as public relations tools than as what they should be: true drivers of business excellence. Part of the problem is that many leaders seem to believe that these statements are somehow the end-product of a process, when in reality they are only the beginning of one.

To get tangible outcomes from vision, mission and value statements, it is important first to understand what they are intended to do:

Vision
An organisation's vision is concerned with its future.
It is about what the organisation wants to become – a snapshot of what excellence will look like.

Mission
If the vision relates to the end of the journey, then the mission is all about the journey itself. In broad terms, it describes how the organisation will operate in relation to its key stakeholders: customers, employees, owners and the wider community.

Values
Values describe what really matters to the organisation as it seeks to live its mission and achieve its vision. These stated values help to bring the hoped-for culture to life by expressing what concerns those working in the business.

The initial value in developing these statements comes from the process of reflection and analysis that goes into developing them. By considering the future and then defining excellence in broad terms, leaders can visualise better what it is they are trying to achieve. Furthermore, by describing the values that matter, they make commitments as to how they will run the organisation, which has implications for organisation culture. However, this is only the first step; the real benefit of vision, mission and values comes from translating them into action.

If vision, mission and values serve as the true driving force for the organisation, they can make a major contribution in guiding the journey to excellence. They allow leaders to benchmark actual achievements against the commitments made in these statements; they allow employees and other stakeholders to measure whether the reality matches the hype. For these reasons, as a leader you should ensure that your approach to developing and living these statements goes beyond the cosmetic exercise seen in so many organisations.

See also

Q76 What is the strategic planning process?
Q78 How should vision, mission and values be developed?
Q79 How should vision, mission and values be used for best effect?

Q78   How should vision, mission and values be developed?

Developing vision, mission and values statements for your organisation is the first step on the road to excellence and should reflect the organisation's intentions. For example, two or three senior leaders sitting in a room developing these statements does not reflect well on the notion of engaging with stakeholders and employees. Therefore, the process taken to develop them should be consultative and participative.

If the organisation is to have real stakeholder focus, leaders should consult with those stakeholders to understand better their expectations. This can be achieved through discussions and focus groups of customers, employees, suppliers and even the wider community if they are deemed to be key stakeholders. The needs of owners usually are clear but they should be defined more clearly than merely to achieve profitability or to maximise return on investment, worthy goals as these may be. The outcome of these discussions inform what is eventually written down in the statements.

In formulating the *vision*, leaders should ask themselves:

- What are we trying to achieve?
- What do we want the organisation to become?
- What would describe 'excellence' for us?
- What is the collective ambition driving us as a leadership team?

When developing the *mission*, leaders should consider:

- What are our customers' expectations and, in turn, what will we deliver for them?
- What will it be about our customer experience that will be unique, that they won't get anywhere else?
- What do our employees mean to us?
- What will it be about working here that stands out from all the places our employees could work?
- What commitments are we making to the wider community?

- What will we deliver for our owners / investors?

Questions such as these help leaders to match what they will deliver to the needs of key stakeholders. Then, it is a matter of formulating broad but compelling statements that give a real flavour of what the organisation is all about.

In particular, when developing the *values* statement, employees can play an important role in helping to contribute to the values that are agreed for the organisation. They might be encouraged to suggest values that are important to them for inclusion in the final statement, which will give them a sense of involvement as well as a degree of ownership. It is always vital to remember that, when individuals feel some ownership for the commitments made on their behalf, they are more likely to strive to live by them.

In setting out to develop the vision, mission and values statements, keep the following points in mind:

- There are no rules as to how to set about the task; be as creative as possible but involve all the relevant stakeholders in the process.
- If broad statements are not your thing, use memorable phrases that have real meaning for you.
- If three statements sounds too unwieldy, just have one, once it incorporates the principles of vision, mission and values.
- If vision, mission and values sound too formal, call them something else – just make sure you end up with 'meaningful sound-bite(s)'.
- Always challenge the organisation to reach new heights but be realistic too: wildly-ambitious or unrealistic statements add little value in the long run.

See also

Q76   What is the strategic planning process?
Q77   Why are organisational vision, mission and values important?
Q79   How should vision, mission and values be used for best effect?

Q79   How should vision, mission and values be used for best effect?

Ultimately, it is what you do with the vision, mission and values statements that counts.

A critical first step in making these statements work for you is to ensure that they are communicated widely and continuously to all key stakeholders. By doing so, as leaders of the organisation, you make your commitments public and create a discipline for yourself; it is always harder to hide from public commitments you have made.

To make a lasting impact on your organisation, the broad sentiments contained in the vision, mission and values statements must be translated into concrete, measurable and time-bound strategic goals, which will be used both to drive performance and to measure achievement. These goals should be stakeholder-focused, so your organisation should have goals relating to:

Owners / investors	A range of financial goals, including return on investment, profitability, earning per share, etc.
Customers	Goals should be defined around customers, including satisfaction and loyalty.
Employees	Goals should be defined that seek to measure engagement levels such as turnover, satisfaction, etc.
Processes	Specific goals should be developed for all key processes, sales and marketing, HR, operations, etc.

By making the vision, mission and values more tangible through the creation of related goals, an organisation starts to bring them to life. Of course, there may be other business goals as well, but the strategic goals should be your driving force.

For these organisational goals, leaders must develop a strategy to realise them. For example, if a strategic goal is to 'increase customer satisfaction by 25% within three years', a clear strategy should be agreed as to how that particular goal is to be achieved; the same principles should be applied for all goals.

With general strategies in place, leaders need to agree specific activities each year to translate those strategies into action. This requires an annual planning process that specifies which steps on the journey to excellence will be implemented in any given year.

Finally, in seeking to use vision, mission and values to best effect, ongoing measurement and feedback is vital to provide information on how well the organisation is doing in terms of achieving its goals and, by correlation, living by its values, implementing its mission and ultimately progressing towards its vision. A comprehensive management information system is required to provide the financial feedback data needed as well as a more holistic view of the business as to how it is meeting the expectations of key stakeholders.

See also

Q76   What is the strategic planning process?
Q77   Why are organisational vision, mission and values important?
Q78   How should vision, mission and values be developed?

Q80   What analysis is important when strategic planning?

Although a major component of strategic planning is concerned with envisioning the future, the present situation cannot be overlooked; how the organisation is currently performing naturally has an impact on all future decisions taken.

Some organisations examine their current position first and then envision the future on that basis. One limitation of this approach is the potential to restrict ambitions; there can be a temptation to set strategic goals at a lower level, in line with current achievements, thereby making their achievement more likely. A better approach is to establish the strategic goals first, then examine the current position and, from that, to build strategies and related plans to bridge the gap from where the organisation is now to where it wants to be. This methodology means that the leaders set their ambitions without being constrained by the current position.

Whatever approach is taken, a comprehensive analysis of the current position is always required as part of strategic planning. Leaders within the organisation must clearly understand the performance dynamics of the *internal environment, the competitive environment and the wider 'macro' environment.* Some data, such as that on internal performance, is readily available, whereas getting information to assess market and competitor performance always is more difficult to find. More challenging still is seeking to gauge economic, social, political or technological trends in the macro environment, as these are susceptible to external forces beyond the control of organisational leaders. However, despite the difficulties in predicting trends in the macro environment beyond the current year, leaders still must make a strong effort to do so, as it is not possible to strategically plan for three to five years ahead without some data to guide the path.

At a more practical level, analysing the current environment means finding answers to important questions such as:

Environment	Sample questions to consider
Internal	• As a leader, you must identify the current strengths and weaknesses of your organisation: • How is your organisation performing financially? • How does that compare to other similar organisations? • Who are your customers? Can you divide them into different key segments? • What are your customers' needs? Are you meeting and more importantly exceeding them? What do your customers think about you at present? How do you know? When customers do give you feedback, how often does the word 'excellent' feature? • How does your product / service offering compare with that of your competitors? Where are the current gaps in what you offer? • Are your employees competent, committed and motivated? Do they play an active or passive role in day to day decision-making? • Are you maximising the use of information technology in your organisation? • Is your organisation considered a leader amongst your competitive set?
Competitive	• Here, you are trying to get a better feel for the dynamics of the markets you operate (or could operate) in: • Do you have a lot of competitors, or only a few? • Are you operating in a mass market, or do you offer a specialist or niche experience? • Is overall demand growing, or subsiding in your region? • Is it easy to set up a comparable business in your area, or are there significant barriers to entry? • What drives the market(s) that you are in? Price, quality or both? What trends are you seeing in your markets? Are you increasing market share or losing it in your key markets? • How does the market operate? Do customers buy directly, online or through intermediaries, or all three? Who are these intermediaries and what relationships do you have with them? • How is technology affecting the market dynamics? • What are the key trends in the industry within which you operate? • What are the overall projections for the industry in your country / region?

Environment	Sample questions to consider
	• What supports are available for organisations such as yours? Are you maximising your usage of those supports? • Who are the main business associations? Do you have a relationship with them?
Macro	• Here, you are looking at general economic and social trends that may impact on your organisation, either in the short or long term: • What is the general economic outlook like for the short and medium term where you are? What is it like in the places where your customers come from? • How are consumer habits / needs changing? What implications might such changes have for you in the short and medium term? • Are there any regulations on the horizon which might have implications for the operation of your business? What do you need to do to get ready for any such legislation/regulations? • What are the future technology developments that will impact on organisations generally in your field? How might they impact your organisation? • What are the environmental issues that you need to respond to?

By addressing questions such as these, you will have a better idea of the strengths, weaknesses, opportunities and threats facing your business, which you then need to examine to determine how your strategies and plans need to respond to these dimensions, if you are to achieve your strategic goals.

See also

Q76   What is the strategic planning process?

Q81   How can I conduct an effective SWOT analysis?

Q81   How can I conduct an effective SWOT analysis?

Once the research required to support strategic planning has been gathered, you need to evaluate its implications and make decisions accordingly. A well-known tool for facilitating this analysis is the SWOT matrix, which involves summarising:

- The current internal Strengths and Weaknesses of the organisation.
- The Opportunities and Threats it faces in the external business environment.

Frequently, when a SWOT analysis is being compiled in an organisation, leaders and other senior personnel gather together; through general discussion, a full SWOT is then prepared. Unfortunately, many of the decisions taken in these circumstances tend to be based on opinion, not fact. Where hard data is used, usually it is to compare current year performance with previous years to give an indication whether some aspect of organisational performance is a strength or a weakness. Usually, there is little or no comparison of the organisation's performance against competitors, industry norms or best-in-class organisations. Worse still, opportunities or threats are often plucked out of thin air, based on collective opinion or 'group-think'. This is completely the wrong way to go about compiling an effective SWOT.

Leaders in an organisation might identify that employee turnover had dropped by 5% in the previous year and, from that, draw the conclusion that this meant they had a dedicated team as a strength. But any aspect of organisational performance, or a particular set of data, only can be evaluated fully based on external comparisons; for example, if the industry norm for employee turnover for that year was a 10% fall, 5% represents underperformance. Worse still, if a leading peer enterprise had reduced turnover by 20% in the past year, then this particular organisation is significantly behind the best performers. And so a perceived strength is really a weakness.

This simple example highlights that, when seeking to identify strengths and weaknesses for inclusion in SWOT analysis, you must keep the following points in mind:

- A SWOT based on opinions is of little value; facts are needed.
- Internal comparison of performance results from year to year, whilst helpful, is not enough; external comparisons are needed and particularly against organisations considered leaders in your field.

The same principle applies when trying to pinpoint opportunities and threats. In particular, in these areas, detailed research often is needed before something can be classified as a real opportunity for the organisation. Remember, if a competitor is better placed to respond to that potential opportunity than you are, then what you thought was an opening for you actually might be a threat. Do the research first, then make the judgement calls.

See also

Q76 What is the strategic planning process?
Q80 What analysis is important when strategic planning?

Q82   How should I develop and implement strategy?

No matter how well-designed and well-communicated your vision, mission, values and strategic goals are, they still add little or no long-term value to your organisation unless you do something to achieve them. Once you identify strategic goals, based on your vision and mission, you must decide what you intend to do in order to realise them.

Another way to look at strategic planning is to think of it as being a funnel that is wide at the top and narrower, or more specific, at the bottom:

Vision, Mission & Values
⇩
Strategic Goals
⇩
Strategy
⇩
Plans
⇩
Results/Outcomes

Many leaders are daunted by strategy and it is often considered something only a CEO or a highly-paid consultant can do. Of course, external guidance is always useful when developing strategy and, yes, finding a winning strategy is never easy but do not be daunted by it on a conceptual level.

Strategy is essentially about the choices an organisation makes, or options it takes, designed to help it move from its current position *(where are we now?)* towards the goals it wants to achieve *(where do we want to be?)*. Strategy should help the organisation play to its strengths, address weaknesses, capitalise on opportunities and prepare for threats. In reality, any organisation usually has a number of integrated strategies in order to achieve each set of the stakeholder-focused goals it has defined.

In light of this, as a leader, you need to consider the strategic goals and then reflect on the alternatives available to help you achieve them. Clearly, the strategies you adopt depend upon your specific strategic goals and the current position of your organisation but will always involve decision-making. A strategy for achieving financial goals might involve choosing between entering a new market, or expanding within the current one; it might involve designing and launching new products, or looking at how to improve the marketing and promotion of the existing product line. For employee-related goals, it could involve redesigning the training and development process, or choosing how to restructure the ways in which performance is rewarded. For customer-related goals, it might involve choices between building up direct sales or moving to online distribution. Strategy is always about choices and decisions and, with the right information, experience and indeed, some gut-feeling, you can do it.

When you have decided upon your general strategies, you need to implement them. Most organisations do so as part of the annual planning process. Any organisation, regardless of size, should prepare an annual business plan, with financial, marketing, human resources and operational components. There are many things to be planned in any given year but specific actions aimed at implementing the strategies must be prioritised, planned and budgeted for annually; otherwise, you get 'drift', which can prove fatal in terms of realising strategic goals.

See also

Q76   What is the strategic planning process?
Q77   Why are organisational vision, mission and values important?
Q78   How should vision, mission and values be developed?
Q79   How should vision, mission and values be used for best effect?
Q83   How can I review strategic effectiveness?

Q83 How can I review strategic effectiveness?

Measuring strategic effectiveness means tracking progress towards your strategic goals. This will tell you whether you are living your mission and moving closer to your ultimate vision. It means measuring progress, analysing the implications of the results you get and taking action to improve.

Measuring strategic effectiveness has two components:

- **Implementation:** Measuring implementation is relatively straightforward in that it involves monitoring (through weekly, monthly and quarterly reviews) whether the actions agreed in the annual business plan to implement your strategy have been put in place. After all, if the action is not taken, then you definitely will not see the results you want.

- **Impact:** Measuring impact is more complex but, in principle, should not be overly difficult. Consider the following points:
  - Have you devised specific performance metrics related to each of your strategic goals? These should include financial measures as well as customer, employee and community-related measures. Many organisations today create a 'dashboard' of key performance measures that are continuously tracked or they use the Balanced Scorecard, which identifies key measures across core dimensions of organisational performance.
  - Do you have the right information systems to give you accurate data, when you need it? Most organisations today have very strong financial information systems but you might need to consider how effective the current approaches are in areas such as gathering customer or employee feedback.
  - At what intervals will you take snapshot measurements? Obviously, financial and market data might be tracked constantly but, for customer or employee satisfaction levels, the intervals might be quarterly, half-yearly or annually.
  - How will you compare your results externally to determine how they measure up to industry norms and, more importantly, against best in class organisations?

- Who is involved in analysing the data? Have you a core team of leaders, with appropriate expertise across all business dimensions, who collectively review performance and make decisions accordingly? This analysis phase also requires you to investigate root causes to ensure you identify the right issues and do not focus on symptoms of more fundamental problems.

Based on what you learn from the review of strategic effectiveness, then plan for the next period to make improvements so that you either address problems identified or build on good performance seen to date. In some cases, you might be forced to re-examine your strategies, or maybe even to conclude that the strategic goals you set were simply overly-ambitious in the first place.

Also as part of your review of strategic effectiveness, over time you will be able to identify trends in your key measures and this will help you to determine whether you are consistently improving and achieving excellence.

See also

Q76   What is the strategic planning process?
Q82   How should I develop and implement strategy?

Q84   What is a leadership competence model?

At best, 'leadership' is a vague term, with different connotations for different people depending upon their perspective. Certainly, in seeking to enhance the quality of leadership in your organisation, you need to be more specific as to what you want leaders to do in order for them to be described as 'effective'. For a long time, organisations relied on job descriptions for leaders and, whilst this is accepted practice, the downside of job descriptions is they focus more on what an individual is expected to *do*, than what they are expected to *achieve*. Thus, more and more organisations are looking at leadership competence models.

Despite the formal undertones associated with a 'competence model', they simply highlight the key areas a leader should focus on and, more importantly, define what they are expected to deliver in those areas. For this reason, they differ widely between organisations; although what all leaders should do is broadly similar regardless of location, each organisation may want their leaders to prioritise different areas for achievement.

In setting out to devise a leadership competence model, or leadership profile, the first consideration is to define the key performance areas for a leader that matter most in your organisation. In its simplest form, leaders must deliver in certain areas:

- **Job-related:** Achieving specific results in relation to their job, which might include increasing sales, reducing costs, increasing customer satisfaction, reducing employee turnover and so on.
- **People-related:** Achieving a whole range of outcomes in relation to their people, such as setting a positive example, motivating their team, or handling conflict efficiently.
- **Process-related:** Achieving results in relation to the process for which they are responsible, such as planning effectively, managing resources, providing training for their people, sustaining quality and so on.

By focusing on these three areas, you can devise not only competences within each but, more importantly, you can specify the results you expect in terms of each competence.

An extract from a basic competence model might look as follows:

Area		Sample Competence		Sample Outcomes
Job-related	→	Achieve revenue targets	→	Increase sales by 10% this year.
	→	Reduce costs	→	Reduce administration costs by €5,000 this year.
	→	Increase customer satisfaction	→	Improve customer feedback score by 5 percentage points this year.
	→	Increase employee satisfaction	→	Raise departmental score in annual employee survey from 75% to 80% satisfaction.
People-related	→	Self-motivation and leadership by example	→	Continuously show *self-motivation* and lead by example.
	→	Energy and enthusiasm	→	Demonstrate high levels of *energy* and *enthusiasm*.
	→	Concern for employees	→	Show *concern* for team-members and interact with them in a positive manner.
Process-related	→	Quality and continuous improvement	→	Achieve a minimum of 90% in all quarterly internal quality audits.
	→	Training, coaching and development	→	Provide the equivalent of 2 hours training per employee per month.
	→	Health and safety management	→	Reduce number of accidents within their area by 50% over last year.

These are just samples of the type of competences that might be in a model. Not only are the specific competences identified, but outcomes for each are highlighted. The achievement of some of these outcomes is easily measured as they relate to hard data, whereas others might be measured through a leader's annual appraisal or from the employee satisfaction survey results received from their team. For that reason, leadership appraisal forms and the headings in the employee satisfaction survey should be aligned with those in the competence model as far as is possible in order to facilitate the measurement process.

See also

Q16   What personal attributes are required to be a successful leader?
Q32   What are the different leadership styles?
Q35   What are the core leadership skills that contribute to success?
Q100 How might I unify all the principles of leadership?

Q85   How can I establish an effective system to manage human resources in the organisation?

In many organisations, particularly small and medium-sized enterprises, the importance of human resources as a key process that supports the achievement of strategic goals still is overlooked today. In some cases, there is not really a human resource process in place at all, rather a personnel management system focused more on legal compliance, recruitment and the various administration tasks linked to managing employees. Important as all these considerations are, human resources must be seen as a key strategic function which, if owned and managed correctly, can help an organisation to realise its vision and deliver on its mission and values statements.

In seeking to establish an effective system within your organisation, you should review whether your existing approach adequately addresses the areas shown in the diagram.

Everything that is required to effectively manage human resources in an organisation is addressed within one of these 11 sub-processes. More importantly, the role is defined as being more strategic in nature as it is concerned with manpower planning to meet organisational needs and other critical areas such as internal communications or managing and monitoring satisfaction levels. Clearly, the individual selected to own and lead this process requires a breadth and depth of talent that surpasses what a 'Personnel Manager' would have. Equally, for HR to truly add strategic value, the post-holder must be seen as a senior leader in the organisation and have direct and ongoing involvement in the strategic planning process.

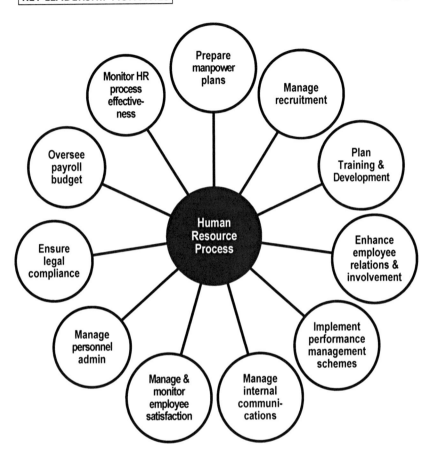

See also

Q75 How do I achieve excellence in my organisation?

Q86   What is employee engagement?

Employee engagement is another example of how buzzwords find their way into management thinking. Although it is a recent term, it can hardly be classified as being a totally new idea. The need for leaders to be focused on issues such as motivation, empowerment, employee satisfaction and productivity is well-established and engagement can be described as an umbrella concept under which all of these concerns fall. However, it moves beyond a narrow focus on generating high satisfaction levels amongst employees because it is more concerned with translating that satisfaction into higher productivity and better performance in order to optimise the contribution that employees make, individually and collectively, to the achievement of strategic goals.

For most leaders, an engaged employee is an individual who is fully committed to the organisation, its vision and mission and is continuously striving to use their talents and raise their productivity to help achieve the organisation's goals. They do so because, in large part, they feel a strong connection between their own goals and those of the organisation. Such characters exist in real life, although research shows that they are in the minority. However, the same research demonstrates that most people have the potential for greater engagement, if the conditions within the organisation are right. Developing truly engaged employees means paying attention to anything that can positively or negatively impact on individual and collective performance.

Many of the studies in this area also have shown that higher engagement levels contribute directly to overall organisational performance, so this is an aspect of organisational and personal leadership worth all the attention you can give it.

Some argue that the larger the organisation, the harder it is to engage employees; this may be of concern to you as a leader if you find yourself in such an environment. While it is undoubtedly more challenging in a larger organisation to fully engage employees, size is not the predominant issue here; engagement has more to do with cultural issues and the range of practices and procedures adopted that influence an employee's daily experience. If a leader of any business is not concerned with employee engagement, they will experience high levels of disengagement, regardless of size. In any case, if each leader within a larger organisation did the right things, they would further engage their own people and the collective effective of that effort would be higher engagement across the organisation.

See also

Q52 How can I motivate and engage my team-members better?
Q87 How can I increase employee engagement levels?
Q88 How might I measure employee engagement?

Q87   How can I increase employee engagement levels?

The 12 factors below are highlighted in various research studies as contributors to employee engagement. They provide a good starting point for you as a leader to reflect on what you can do to raise engagement levels amongst those employees who report to you.

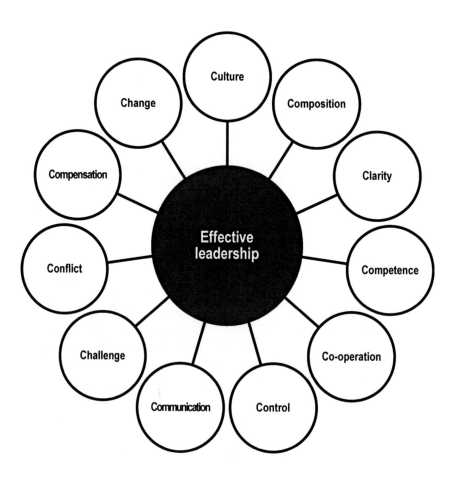

Some general points to note on each of the circles in the diagram:

- **Effective leadership:** Without effective leadership, engagement levels will not be as high as they could potentially be, regardless of what is happening in the other factors. An employee's willingness to engage is enhanced or reduced depending upon the nature of their relationship with their boss.

- **Culture:** While there is no 'right' culture, certain environments build engagement, whereas others do the opposite. All leaders play an important role in building a culture that draws employees in rather than pushes them away.

- **Composition:** You must pay close attention to how you recruit people into your existing team. Employees do not necessarily all have to like each other, nor will they, but there must be a general 'fit' between all members; otherwise, it is hard to engage them because who wants to work alongside people with whom you have little or nothing in common.

- **Clarity:** In this context, clarity means ensuring that your employees understand both aspirations and expectations. Aspirations relate to the big picture and, as a basic building block of engagement, you need to help employees to understand fully where the organisation is going and how they can contribute to that. Clarity also is required on what is expected of employees, as nothing destroys engagement faster than conflicting directions or shifting responsibilities.

- **Competence:** Most employees want to build their skills and talents at work, so you need to ensure that there are relevant and regular opportunities for personal development. Equally, all employees should be similarly competent at what they are expected to do. If not, others in the team have to take up the slack, which creates resentment, or worse still conflict, and chips away at engagement.

- **Co-operation:** Levels of co-operation in teams are both a driver of engagement and a reflection of it. When people work well together, they build bonds and trust increases and this, in turn, improves general engagement levels.

- **Control:** Controlling how individuals behave within teams is critical to engagement because, when some team-members are allowed to step out of line without consequence, it de-motivates engaged employees who question why they should bother. Equally, too controlling an environment stifles engagement because people sense a lack of freedom and autonomy.

- **Communication:** This is always key to the levels of engagement. Where communication is regular, open, two-way and, more importantly, effective, employees tend to be more engaged.

- **Challenge:** For most employees, having a sense of challenge in their work is vital to how engaged they feel with the organisation. When work feels repetitive or mundane, employees naturally feel less engaged, so you need continuously to find ways to challenge them.

- **Conflict:** The manner in which conflict is managed can have a major impact on how engaged employees are likely to be. Constructive conflict, which leads to new ideas and better solutions, should be encouraged, but managed, so that employees feel that they can speak their minds or contribute appropriately. Destructive conflict, on the other hand, adds no value and should be dealt with promptly by the leader; failure to do so impacts on engagement levels, as most people hate to work in a poisoned atmosphere.

- **Compensation:** In the broadest sense, this is about people feeling rewarded for the contribution they make. Pay and conditions, of course, are an important element in this, but constructive feedback and positive recognition, when deserved, are just as powerful.

- **Change:** How change is managed also can impact on the levels of engagement. Too little change can result in stagnation, which destroys engagement, yet too much of it, or too much meaningless change, simply frustrates employees and causes them to disengage.

Depending upon your level in the organisation, you may have more or less influence over some of these factors. However, most should be directly within your control and you should spend time now reflecting on how well each of them currently contributes to the levels of engagement within your organisation and where you can begin to make improvements.

See also

Q52   How can I motivate and engage my team-members better?

Q86   What is employee engagement?

Q88   How might I measure employee engagement?

Q88 How might I measure employee engagement?

Measuring employee engagement means focusing initially on the distinction between a satisfied and an engaged employee. Even though an employee may be generally satisfied with their job and the organisation, there is no guarantee that they will commit more or work harder as a result. For sure, it is an indicator but not necessarily a guarantee. Some well-known engagement surveys define specific criteria that are recognised as being drivers of engagement and provide questions to employees against those criteria.

At an informal level, as leader you can measure engagement levels on a continuous basis simply by monitoring ongoing performance; there will always be indicators to support you in this. For example, if you measure productivity in your field of business, then a drop in that indicator could have something to do with engagement levels; so too might a fall in customer satisfaction levels or an increase in employee turnover.

To develop a more formal approach, and to align with the 12 drivers of engagement (**Q87**), develop your own employee engagement survey around these drivers to measure employee satisfaction and engagement levels at the same time.

Taking three of the drivers – leadership, culture and composition – as an example, this might work as follows:

Factor		Potential outcomes
Leadership	→	Employees have a positive impression of leadership within the organisation.
	→	Employees genuinely feel valued and respected by their leaders.
Culture	→	Employees feel that the organisation shows general care and concern for their welfare.
	→	Employees like the culture in the organisation and feel proud about working here.

Factor		Potential outcomes
Composition	→	Employees have positive relationships with their colleagues.
	→	Employees respect diversity amongst those they work with and feel respected by others.

Staying with the three drivers, next develop a questionnaire along the following lines, using a simple rating scale: 1 = Disagree Strongly; 2 = Disagree Somewhat; 3 = Neither Agree nor Disagree; 4 = Agree Somewhat; 5 = Agree Strongly. In the sample below, there are three statements for each of the three sample drivers. The first two in each section relate to the outcomes described above and measure satisfaction levels, while the third italicised statement measures whether that satisfaction is translated in higher engagement levels.

Factor	Possible statements	Rating				
		1	2	3	4	5
Leadership	Leadership in this organisation is highly effective					
	The way I am treated by my leaders makes me feel valued and respected					
	How I am led maximises my willingness to commit fully to my job					
Culture	Leaders in this organisation genuinely care about my welfare					
	The culture here makes me feel proud to work in this organisation					
	I like the culture in this organisation and this encourages me to put more effort into my job					
Composition	There are positive working relationships within my team and we are mutually respectful to each other					
	Diversity and difference is embraced in my team					
	The mix of people in my team works well and brings the best out in me					

Although only a sample approach, this shows how the 12 drivers of engagement can be used as the basis for an effective survey to measure both employee satisfaction and engagement levels.

See also

Q52   How can I motivate and engage my team-members better?
Q86   What is employee engagement?
Q87   How can I increase employee engagement levels?

Q89 How can I establish a leadership mentoring programme within the organisation?

Positive mentoring relationships have the potential to bring tangible benefits for the individuals concerned and, more importantly, for the organisation. The concept of mentoring is not new, and informal mentoring relationships always have been an important element in leadership development. However, today, many organisations are attempting to harness the power of mentoring in a more formal manner.

Formalising a framework to support effective mentoring within an organisation has been shown to enhance employee performance but also serves to build stronger relationships across the wider leadership team. It is successful for many reasons, including:

- It offers a flexible approach.
- It is people-centred in its approach.
- It balances organisational and individual needs.
- It allows for two-way communication.
- It has a broad development focus.
- It can aid succession planning.
- It focuses on Individual needs.

Successful mentoring programmes have many advantages, but the process is not without risks. Without real commitment from both mentors and mentees, as well as a viable structure and defined logistics, the initiative is likely to fail and may do more harm than good. Therefore, in developing a mentoring programme, you need to consider four interdependent dimensions:

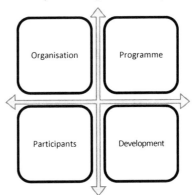

- Organisation
  - Does the culture of the organisation support the mentoring concept?
  - Are there already strong relationships between senior and more junior leaders?
  - Will the organisation provide the necessary resources and support to underpin the mentoring programme?
- Programme
  - What are the specific goals for the programme?
  - What will the programme entail?
  - How will mentors and mentees be matched up?
  - How long will the programme last?
- Participants
  - Will the mentors and the mentees be committed to the concept?
  - Do the mentors have the required 'mentoring' skills at present?
- Development
  - How will the tangible developmental outcomes for each individual be defined?
  - How will their needs be met by the mentoring programme?

Also recognise that, although the likely mentors – senior leaders – already have the skills, knowledge and experience that will be of benefit to the more junior leaders, they may not necessarily have the appropriate talents and qualities required to develop an effective mentoring relationship. A successful mentor requires many personal attributes to enable them to create a positive mentoring environment. In conjunction with these skills, the mentor must possess a broad understanding of adult psychology and behaviour, as well as highly effective communication skills. In developing a programme, consider these issues.

The key steps in developing a mentoring programme are shown in the diagram below.

After one full cycle of the mentoring programme, it may be necessary to adjust aspects of it, depending upon outcomes. For the second cycle, it is advisable to rotate mentors and mentees to facilitate broader learning and relationship-building.

See also

Q48 How might I use mentoring and networking as tools to help me grow as a leader?

Q90   What is performance management?

Performance management is a broad field and includes any activity you might undertake as a leader that is designed to ensure that personal and organisational goals are consistently achieved; most of your day-to-day activities make some contribution to the performance management effort.

Performance management occurs at a number of levels as shown in the diagram:

- The effectiveness of an organisation in achieving its goals must be monitored and managed.

- Performance across the various departments, functions and processes must be evaluated on a continuous basis.

- Individual performance of all employees must be monitored constantly in both formal and informal ways.

Although performance management often is limited to the management of individual performance, it is important to recognise that it has to do with both the individual and the organisation (strategic and operational aspects). In any case, improving individual performance in turn will positively impact on overall organisational performance.

Key elements of performance management
Performance management, at whatever level, is a continuous process and, although the particular activities involved vary somewhat depending upon the nature of the performance being measured, there are general activities applicable to all:

- **Set goals and targets:** At a strategic level, this relates to setting the strategic goals whereas, at the organisational level, this means setting particular targets for various departments, functions or processes and, for individuals, means setting personal objectives.

- **Communicate goals and targets:** Regardless of the nature of the goals and targets, they must always be communicated to ensure that those involved in achieving them are clear on expectations.

- **Implementation:** At a strategic level, this may involve evaluating the current position or defining strategies to realise the goals. For specific functions or processes, this might mean developing plans, setting standards and managing day-today activities. For the individual, this could include providing training and development, coaching and mentoring to support them in the achievement of their targets.

- **Monitoring ongoing performance:** The principles of monitoring performance at all levels are the same, although timeframes may vary. Monitoring strategic progress may require quarterly, half-yearly or annual analysis; at organisational level, performance is monitored at all times and weekly and monthly data can be used to track progress; while individual progress is tracked continuously by a leader and may include periodic job-chats or evaluations.

- **Measure progress formally:** Although all progress is monitored on an ongoing basis, formal measurement at strategic and organisational levels can occur at defined periods and, specifically, during the planning process for the coming year when detailed analysis of current year performance is undertaken. In terms of the individual, there is usually an annual appraisal that tracks formally how well they have delivered on expectations.

- **Recognise achievement and identify areas for improvement:** The outcome from any measurement activity always should be to recognise achievements and, at strategic level, senior leader rewards are usually linked to those achievements. Failure to achieve strategic goals and targets will require detailed analysis and corrective action to resolve the problem. Equally, at organisational and individual levels, actual performance against targets can guide reward schemes, help to identify areas for improvement and influence the goals established for the following period.

Whatever your current level as a leader, you will be involved in some way in managing organisational and individual performance, so it comprises a significant proportion of what you do. The performance management cycle highlighted here can be applied regardless of context.

See also

Q75   How do I achieve excellence in my organisation?
Q92   What is process mapping and how can it help improve business performance?
Q93   How can I improve service delivery in the organisation?

Q91 Why is succession planning important?

Succession planning is not an everyday concern, although you should not ignore it because it has major implications for long-term sustainability. Often, succession planning in an organisational context is limited to senior leaders but it has direct relevance at all levels.

Succession planning involves identifying roles that are deemed critical for the smooth and effective running of the organisation and then creating systems and processes that help to identify and develop potential successors for the people currently holding the posts. Thus, succession planning has implication for policies and procedures in areas, such as:

- Recruitment and selection.
- Training and development.
- Rewards and recognition.
- Compensation.
- Promotion.
- Mentoring.

The aim of any organisation should be to achieve a level of succession planning where there are employees in place at any given time who can step into vital positions. Of course, the realities of the working environment means that this is not always possible and there is always a case to be made for external recruitment but, as far as is practical, organisations should promote from within and then recruit to fill the lower positions left vacant. This provides for greater continuity and offers potential career paths for individuals, which in turn serves as part of the attraction when seeking to retain high-performers at all levels.

Key considerations when seeking to maximise the potential for succession planning include:

Effective succession planning also has another benefit that is often overlooked. By preparing individuals to step into the shoes of others, you create a more competitive environment within the organisation. Once this is well managed, it can raise overall performance as key individuals recognise the need to exceed expectations continually.

See also

Q67   How should I retain my best employees?
Q89   How can I establish a leadership mentoring programme within the organisation?

Q92 What is process mapping and how can it help improve business performance?

Process mapping is a way of depicting key work processes in visual format in order to support decision-making around improving efficiency and facilitate continuous improvement. Key steps in process mapping include:

- **Identify key processes:** Regardless of the nature of your organisation, key processes are likely to include: strategic planning; leadership; quality management; financial management; human resources; facilities management; environmental management and managing innovation. Additional processes vary by organisation but may include: marketing; customer relationship management; and various operational or administrative processes.

- **Assign ownership and map processes:** Each process should have an owner. For functional processes such as Human Resources, this is usually the individual holding that post. However, for other processes such as Quality Management or Managing Innovation which may be cross-functional, it may be necessary to assign individual responsibility for these areas; in such cases, this often can be allocated to a high-performing employee with some expertise in the given area as opposed to recruiting or creating a new post.

- **Process mapping:** Process mapping itself should be led by the process owner but should include input from their team and consultation with others across the organisation. It is critical that the maps accurately depict how the process actually works in practice currently. In developing the maps, major activities must be identified first and then sub-tasks defined within each of these broad areas of activity. An example of what a basic process map might look like for Marketing is shown in the first diagram below. This may not be an exhaustive list of major activities in marketing but there is enough in the diagram to demonstrate the first step in process mapping.

Next, for each of the key activities, the process owner and their team should define the sub-tasks within each. For the 'Conduct Market Research' activity, these might include the sub-tasks shown in the diagram below:

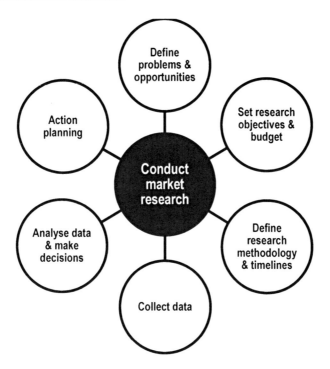

Each of these sub-tasks then may be broken down further into specific steps. Mapping all key activities, sub-tasks and steps fully gives a clear picture, not only of what is involved in a particular process, but also of what a process owner is responsible for leading. There is also value for all concerned in process mapping as it makes them reflect thoroughly on what it is they do.

- **Identifying and implementing improvements:** The true value of process mapping in this context only is seen if the exercise leads to enhanced performance of the process. To do this, a process owner and their team should identify where improvements can be made; instead of asking broad questions, "how can we improve our marketing?", they can be more focused on a particular key activity and examine how its sub-tasks and related steps can be enhanced. By adopting this approach for all key activities and sub-tasks, the collective result will be an enhanced marketing process.

- **Measuring improvements:** To demonstrate the impact of improvements made, define key performance measures for a process overall, and for many of its key activities. By tracking these measures, you will have concrete evidence to demonstrate improvements in a particular process.

See also

Q90   What is performance management?

Q93 How can I improve service delivery in the organisation?

Achieving excellence in service delivery is one of the great challenges for all leaders who operate within service-oriented organisations. Even if your leadership role does not bring you into direct contact with clients, you still have internal customers to worry about, so the principles described here are as applicable in that context.

Leaders set the foundation for improving service delivery when they develop the vision and mission, for it is here that you first publicise your commitments to the customer. The general commitments that you make in those statements should serve as the bedrock of all your efforts in delivering service excellence; it is a matter of aligning all service-orientated activities against those principles. Easier said than done, of course, but without the foundation in place, your efforts will lack focus.

All organisations promote the idea that they are customer-focused but few really achieve that goal. In identifying ways in which you can enhance service delivery, it is important to do so in line with the customer service journey, which starts with their *expectations*, then customers have the *experience* of what you offer, and following that they make an *evaluation* of that experience based on their expectations. This process applies to both internal and external customers. The customer journey can be a valuable tool to use in order to structure better how you manage customer service within your organisation. Focus on the following questions, and develop appropriate responses based on the answers you find.

Expectations	Experience	Evaluation
How well do you really know your customers?	Physical: If your customers come on-site to experience your service, how well does the quality of your physical facilities match expectations?	Are you meeting, and better still exceeding, your customers' expectations?
What are your customers' common and specific expectations?		How do you know? How effective are your feedback mechanisms?
What systems / structures do you have in place to give you that information?	Product / Services: Are the products and services that you offer consistently of a high standard?	How is customer feedback analysed and used to guide improvements?
How often do you hold focus groups or research the changing needs of your customers?	People: Do your people have a real service mindset?	Can you pinpoint any service improvements made in the past three months that were directly based on customer feedback? If not, why not?
	Procedures: Do you have defined procedures in place to ensure consistency, quality and efficiency in service delivery?	

By reflecting on these fundamental questions, you may identify some areas where you can further improve, even if you are performing at a high level already.

See also

Q77   Why are organisational vision, mission and values important?
Q90   What is performance management?

Q94 How can I apply the principles of continuous improvement within the organisation?

A common feature of all successful individuals and organisations is a capacity for self-improvement. Part of the ability to push constantly for better performance is undoubtedly an individual's mindset or the collective philosophy of organisational leaders but having a defined structure in place to facilitate continuous improvement is also an important factor; it will not happen by accident. Note also that periodic improvement is not the same thing as continuous improvement.

Key elements in any continuous improvement process include:

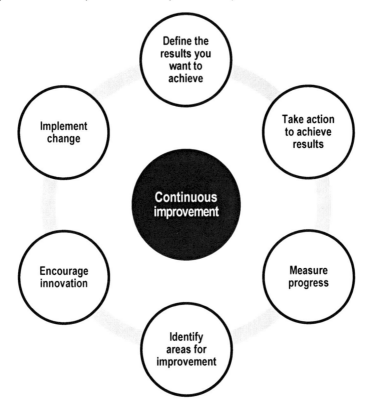

In any attempt to improve, at any level of the organisation, there has to be clear definition of the expected results. Without defining expectations in measurable terms, how can progress be gauged?

The key to continuous improvement is to use your measures to identify where problems lie. Then, in addressing these problems, it is important to use your process for managing innovation, as it is only through innovation that you can find new ideas and better ways of doing things.

See also

Q90   What is performance management?
Q96   How can I encourage and manage innovation?

Q95 What is benchmarking and why is it important?

Benchmarking, the activity of comparing your organisation's processes and performance against industry norms and best practices, is a critical concept for all leaders in organisations. It has a role to play in strategic planning, innovation, continuous improvement and even performance management. Benchmarking can happen informally – the best leaders are always on the look-out for new ways of doing things – but it also should be formalised and structured, so that it is not seen as something to be done occasionally but instead is a key process within the organisation.

Effective benchmarking can deliver significant benefits for an organisation, both in enhancing the skills of individuals and in allowing a more accurate assessment of how the organisation is performing than can otherwise be achieved through internal measurement and analysis alone. It can also help to confirm that an organisation is achieving excellence.

There are two main types of benchmarking:

- **Benchmarking results:** When an organisation benchmarks its key performance results against peers and world class businesses, those results begin to have more relevance. Improvements seen in sales, reductions in costs or positive results in areas such as customer and employee satisfaction take on new meaning when benchmarked; they are shown either to be at the leading edge or lagging behind the norm. As a leader, this provides you with essential information in terms of planning for better results in the future. However, when benchmarking results, ensure you do so on true like-for-like comparisons.

- **Benchmarking processes:** Benchmarking also can deliver a positive contribution to improved performance by comparing how you manage a particular process against how that process is managed in other companies, particularly those deemed to excel in that particular area. However, benchmarking your processes is more than a 'site visit to have a look around' and should be structured to deliver tangible end-results. In addition, team-based approaches to benchmarking are more effective, as they allow for clearer identification of the purpose of the benchmarking activity and greater sharing of learning as a result.

A team established to benchmark a particular process should consider the following:

- **What aspect of the process is to be benchmarked?** It is difficult to benchmark an entire process at one time; it is better for the team to identify specific activities within that process (usually, those that are underperforming) to be benchmarked. Specifically, the team must clarify what problems or issues they expect to get insights into by benchmarking.

- **Which organisation to choose to benchmark against?** For the exercise to have any real value, you should benchmark against an organisation that performs well in the particular areas under consideration – better still if you can benchmark against the leader(s) in that field. Once the company is selected, make contact to see whether they are willing to share their knowledge and, if so, to arrange the logistics of the benchmarking visit.

- **How to structure the visit?** To get the most out of the visit, there should be a clear agenda prepared in agreement with the benchmarking partner; the team should have their specific questions and be clear on what they want to see in practice.

- **What to do with the information gained from the visit?** Many organisations fall into the trap of trying to copy best practices they see in other operations. This rarely is effective because to do so ignores the culture and context that helped to generate the excellent results seen. Therefore, as the old saying goes, it is better to adapt, not adopt, and the team should explore how the principles learned can be applied in your organisation.

For all key processes in an organisation, key performance measures should track how effective a particular process is. And, when improvements are made as a result of benchmarking, the impact of those changes should be reflected in the relevant measures over time.

See also

Q94 How can I apply the principles of continuous improvement within the organisation?

Q96 How can I encourage and manage innovation?

Q96   How can I encourage and manage innovation?

Finding and exploiting new ideas for competitive advantage is another important aspect of any leadership role. To be truly innovative, you need a defined process for managing the identification and implementation of better ways of doing things; this goes far beyond the placing of a suggestion box in the staff canteen, actually a sign of lack of creativity in itself.

To encourage innovation, recognise that it cannot happen in isolation. In addition to structuring it as an activity, what really drives innovation is having leaders and employees who are fully engaged and have a real commitment to be the best at what they do. Without this, the potential for innovation will be limited or confined to the truly dedicated few. As a leader, you should recognise the inter-connectivity of all aspects of leading people; specifically, the capacity for innovation is dependent upon other factors being in place.

In designing and managing an internal process for innovation and creativity that provides for new ideas and solutions, you must define how that process will work, who will take ownership for it and how ideas will be identified, evaluated and, where appropriate, implemented. Key elements in any process for innovation include:

See also

Q94 How can I apply the principles of continuous improvement within the organisation?

Q95 What is benchmarking and why is it important?

Q97   How should I manage a crisis?

A crisis can hit an organisation at any time, often when least expected. Recent corporate history is littered with examples of how high-profile organisations were rocked, not only by the crisis itself but perhaps more by how poorly they responded to it. In spite of all the resources and expertise available, the media training, and highly-paid public relations consultants, some organisations seem to become overwhelmed by the scale and pace of a crisis. Yet, even smaller scale crises can be damaging for organisations; you do not have to be pumping oil into the Gulf of Mexico to face the potential need for a crisis management response at some point. Failure to cope effectively with crises usually stems from lack of preparation, slow and uncoordinated responses and poor internal and external communications.

Some general guidelines relevant here include:

- **Prevent:** Prevention is always better than cure so, as far as is possible, ensure that you have defined processes in place for risk analysis and that, as an organisation, you are proactive in mitigating those risks. Eradicating or minimising risks is the first step in crisis management.

- **Prepare:** It is not possible to prepare in advance for a crisis; were that the case, it would not be a crisis. However, you can prepare by creating appropriate systems, teams and contingency plans that can be spurred quickly into action regardless of the specific nature of any crisis that may arise – this is your responsibility as a leader.

- **Respond:** The best laid plans and preparations only go so far in helping to improve the state of readiness; when a crisis unfolds, strong leadership is everything. It is critical that the response is swift and effective, based on clear problem definition and geared towards immediate and long term components of the solution. Many failures in crisis management have been linked to a failure of leadership.

- **Communicate:** Any significant crisis attracts media and public attention; therefore, it is critical that the flow of information is managed pro-actively, not re-actively. Losing the public relations battle, even if the crisis is effectively managed, still can lead to reputational damage.

- **Learn:** An important activity, once the crisis has passed, is to identify the lessons learned, highlight successes and shortcomings and integrate that learning into future preparations.

See also

Q45 How can I develop my problem-solving skills?

Q98   How should I lead change for best results?

Change is a feature of life in organisations today and leaders constantly face both small and large changes at work. Consequently, you must be comfortable in dealing with change yourself and in helping your team-members to cope with it, particularly changes that are substantial in nature. For such major changes, you should follow a structured, but not rigid, approach to implementation, taking into account the not inconsequential human relations issues associated with any change. Unfortunately, many leaders mishandle change, which can lead to significant resentment and conflict, much of which is avoidable if some basic principles and processes for managing change are applied.

People and change

In terms of coping with change, as a general rule, the more involvement people have in determining the nature and direction of changes affecting them, the more easily they will buy into and support the implementation process. The reverse is also true, of course; the more powerless they feel over changes directly affecting them, the more resistance you will see. However, even when people cannot input into the decision-making process itself, if they are kept informed and, if possible, involved in determining how best to implement the proposals, that can go some way to alleviating their concerns.

Most people are willing to grasp change readily, depending upon how it is presented and handled. However, there are some who fear it and fight it as much as they can. As a leader, you must recognise the human dimension to handling change, which must be addressed during the implementation process. Better deal with discontent or fear at the outset, than to ignore natural human reactions and be forced to deal with rebellion at a later stage. Often, people go through fairly predictable reactions to change:

Denial → Resistance → Acceptance → Commitment

When you hear "that'll never work here", do not immediately see this as a negative sign; what it often means is "convince me" or "how does this affect me?". Helping your team-members to cope with change often requires a selling process on your behalf, particularly in an environment where there has been ineffective change in the past.

When faced with individual reactions to change, recognise that you cannot move people from Denial to Commitment in a single step. Your initial goal always should be just to deal with people's fears and to get people to try the new approach. If it is for the better, then they will see the benefits and resistance will diminish over time.

Leading the change process

How you lead the change process also plays an important role in the results you get. Try to rush through major change and you will find resentment building up; take too long implementing it, and people grow tired of the uncertainty.

For leading any major change process, the following framework can be helpful:

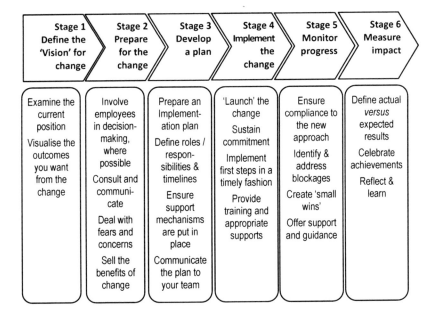

Stage 1 Define the 'Vision' for change	Stage 2 Prepare for the change	Stage 3 Develop a plan	Stage 4 Implement the change	Stage 5 Monitor progress	Stage 6 Measure impact
Examine the current position Visualise the outcomes you want from the change	Involve employees in decision-making, where possible Consult and communicate Deal with fears and concerns Sell the benefits of change	Prepare an Implement-ation plan Define roles / respon-sibilities & timelines Ensure support mechanisms are put in place Communicate the plan to your team	'Launch' the change Sustain commitment Implement first steps in a timely fashion Provide training and appropriate supports	Ensure compliance to the new approach Identify & address blockages Create 'small wins' Offer support and guidance	Define actual *versus* expected results Celebrate achievements Reflect & learn

Following a framework such as this allows you to take the initiative, plan for implementation and remain in control over the process. It helps you to achieve greater 'buy-in' through communicating with, and supporting, your team. It also allows you to define and manage key implementation steps, so that they are more likely to be timely and to deliver positive outcomes.

Keep the following points in mind:

- Change must lead to tangible benefits, if employees are expected to buy into it.
- You must 'sell' the change to your employees.
- Change just for the sake of it winds people up and should be avoided.
- Include your employees in decision-making around change, where possible.
- The bigger the change, the more difficult it can be for employees, so you need to take a strong leadership role in making the change happen.
- The implementation of change should be time-bound, as dragged-out change can be disheartening.
- Make sure you define and communicate clear implementation plans and that deadlines are adhered to.
- Show benefits to your employees as early as possible in the change process, so people see the value of it.
- Offer lots of support and guidance to your employees as they seek to work through the change.
- Recognise that change processes provide ideal opportunities for negative team-members to 'stir things up'. Pay particular attention to the influence they exert at such times.

See also

Q75   How do I achieve excellence in my organisation?

Q99   What is corporate social responsibility?

Corporate social responsibility (CSR) has grown in importance in recent times and, while some organisations stand accused of being more concerned with appearing to be socially responsible than with actually being so, it remains an important consideration for all leaders. CSR involves an organisation striving to be a good corporate citizen by carrying out its functions in a way that has a positive, rather than a negative, impact on stakeholders – be they customers, employees, suppliers, the wider community at large or regulators and government bodies. CSR is of relevance to organisations of all sizes.

Given that organisations are involved in many activities, CSR's many dimensions include:

- Overall governance and ethics.
- Diversity and equality issues.
- Fair and accountable consumer-related practices.
- Effective environmental management.
- Equitable dealings with suppliers.
- Health and safety considerations.
- Open and transparent financial reporting.
- Positive working environment and conditions.

Rather than seeing CSR as something that must be done, you should embrace CSR as a way to run a better, and more profitable, organisation that meets the needs of all stakeholders. The best organisations go far beyond the basic expectations imposed on them under law and see a tremendous return for doing so. For example, by applying CSR principles in terms of human resources, the return for the business will be greater retention of employees and reduced recruitment costs; through more open and honest dealing with consumers, the spin-off will be increased satisfaction and loyalty; by putting in place effective environmental programmes, the organisation not only will contribute positively to the local environment but will see a reduction in its energy and waste management costs. However, to see such positive outcomes, you must ensure that the principles of CSR filter down throughout the organisation into practical measures:

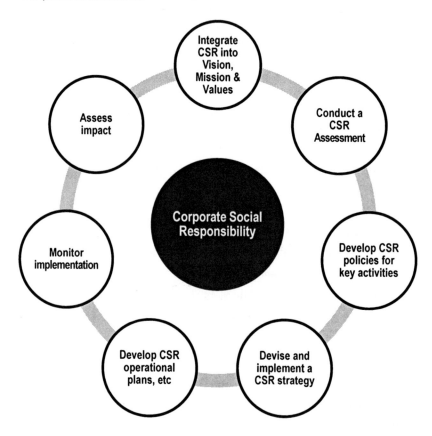

A starting point for any organisation in seeking to adopt CSR principles and practices, of course, is to integrate its general commitments into its vision, mission and values. Next, you should ensure that a full CSR audit is carried out to help define minimum obligations and then to determine which best practices may be applied. As part of this, key stakeholders should be consulted to determine their expectations.

Based on the findings of the audit, a CSR policy should be prepared, or CSR principles integrated into existing policies that chart the organisation's commitments. To implement these policies, a CSR strategy is required, or CSR goals should be integrated into the organisation's overall strategy, which includes defining specific targets related to CSR. And, as with any aspect of strategy, clear plans and programmes must be put in place to achieve the goals. This may include actions such as redesigning some employee-related processes, developing and enhancing environmental management procedures, reviewing supplier relationships or updating health and safety systems within the organisation. Finally, as with any key process, there should be continuous monitoring and measurement not only to determine the impact on stakeholders but also to demonstrate the positive returns generated by CSR for the organisation.

See also

Q77 Why are organisational vision, mission and values important?
Q82 How should I develop and implement strategy?
Q90 What is performance management?
Q94 How can I apply the principles of continuous improvement within the organisation?
Q95 What is benchmarking and why is it important?

Q100   How might I unify all the principles of leadership?

Since 100 questions spanning five important areas might seem independent of one another, it may be useful for you as a leader to visualise how they are interdependent and combine to make you as effective as possible. The diagram demonstrates the relationship between the range of content provided in **QUICK WIN LEADERSHIP**:

- Everything begins with stakeholder focus.

- From that, vision, mission, values are developed, translated into specific goals and strategies are defined to realise the goals.

- Strategy is operationalised through the annual business plan.

- Individual leadership effectiveness, coupled with how well key leadership activities are managed, determines how good an organisation is at realising its goals.

- Evidence to determine this is found through a range of key performance measures, monitored continuously and at defined intervals.

- The lessons learned from those measures support an organisation in its efforts to benchmark and improve continuously.

The diagram below may be helpful to you as you consider how effective your organisation is as a whole, or how good your individual leaders are, or simply as a means to help you reflect on your own performance.

See also

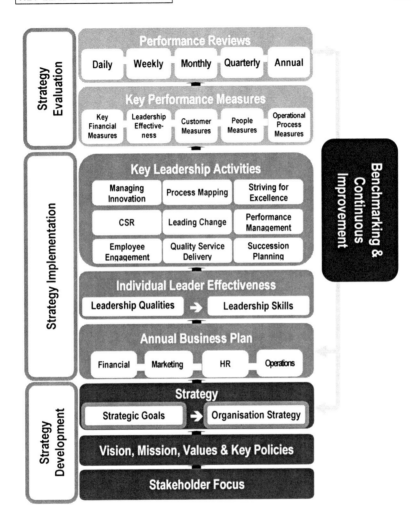

ABOUT THE AUTHOR

Enda Larkin has held a number of senior management positions in Ireland, UK and the US and has worked as a management development consultant since 1994. He has led a variety of consulting projects in the hotel, tourism, aviation and banking sectors throughout Europe and the Middle East and has also designed and delivered numerous leadership programmes; in recent years, he has also specialised in coaching leaders and top executives to maximise their potential as leaders.

He holds a BSc in Management from Trinity College Dublin and an MBA from ESCP-EAP Paris. He is the author of **Ready to Lead?** (Pearson / Prentice Hall), **How to Run a Great Hotel** (How to Books, UK) and **The Impostor Leaders** (to be published in 2011).

He currently lives in Geneva, Switzerland and may be contacted via **www.htc-consult.com** or at **info@htc-consult.com**.

ABOUT THE QUICK WIN SERIES

The **Quick Win** series of books, apps and websites is designed for the modern, busy reader, who wants to learn enough to complete the immediate task at hand, but needs to see the information in context.

Topics published to date include:

- QUICK WIN MARKETING.
- QUICK WIN DIGITAL MARKETING.

Topics planned for 2010 include:

- QUICK WIN B2B SALES.
- QUICK WIN ECONOMICS.
- QUICK WIN LEAN BUSINESS.
- QUICK WIN MEDIA LAW IRELAND.
- QUICK WIN SAFETY MANAGEMENT.
- QUICK WIN SMALL BUSINESS.

For more information, see **www.oaktreepress.com**.

Lightning Source UK Ltd.
Milton Keynes UK
27 October 2010

161993UK00002B/2/P

9 781904 887478